Sewing for Children

35 step-by-step projects to help kids aged 3 and up learn to sew

Emma Hardy

CICO BOOKS

LONDON NEW YORK

This edition published in 2017 by CICO Books
An imprint of Ryland Peters & Small Ltd
20–21 Jockey's Fields   341 E 116th St
London WC1R 4BW   New York, NY 10029

www.rylandpeters.com

10 9 8 7 6 5 4 3 2 1

First published in 2010 by CICO Books

Text © Emma Hardy 2010
Design, illustration, and photography © CICO Books 2010

A CIP catalog record for this book is available from the
Library of Congress and the British Library.

ISBN: 978 1 78249 462 1

Printed in China

Editor: Helen Ridge
Designer: Barbara Zuñiga
Photographer: Debbie Patterson
Illustrators: Stephen Dew and Kate Simunek

Contents

Introduction

Sewing is such a wonderful skill to learn and one that will be useful throughout your life—whether you need to sew a button on a shirt or want to create lovely things for yourself and your home.

I was taught to sew when I was very young and spent many happy hours designing and making clothes for my dolls. Once I had mastered the basic stitches, I loved being able to create things from scraps of fabric and was proud to have made them myself. As I got older, I started to stitch my own clothes and have used my sewing skills in lots of different ways ever since. Now my daughters are learning to sew and are enjoying it just as much as I did.

In this book you will find step-by-step instructions for 35 projects, ranging from very simple spoon puppets to more complicated creations like the lovely rag dolls. You need very few tools and materials to get started and most of the projects take only a couple of hours to complete. Many of the projects would make treasured gifts for family and friends and I hope lots of them inspire boys to sew as well as girls.

There is a handy techniques section to help you with all the basic stitches, which you can either practice on scrap fabric or learn as you go along. Start collecting buttons and ribbons, storing them in jars and pots, and put aside old clothes in great colors and patterns then recycle them into brilliant new creations. There are instructions explaining how to make each project, but as you become more confident you may want to make changes and add your own personal touches, creating designs that are truly unique to you.

There are very few hard and fast rules with sewing—you will find your own way to do things. Try using different fabrics and threads and stitch your own fabulous makes, letting your imagination run riot. Don't worry about your first attempts not being perfect, with practice your stitches will become neater and more even. And remember, you want your sewing to have a wonderful handmade feel so that everyone will know that you stitched it yourself!

Chapter 1

Animals & Other Creatures

Glove Bunny

Transform an old glove into a cute bunny with just a few stitches. Tuck two of the fingers and the thumb inside the glove and stuff it to make the head, before sewing odd buttons on for the face. Use socks to make the legs and finish with a simple dress made from a scrap of fabric, edged in braid for extra decoration.

Materials

Old glove
Scissors
Embroidery floss (thread) and needle
2 buttons
Fiberfill (stuffing)
Old pair of socks
Pins
Needle and thread
Pinking shears
Scrap of fabric for the dress
Braid or bobble fringe
Ribbon for the bow

1. Take the glove and push the two middle fingers and the thumb down inside it. Cut a length of embroidery floss (thread) and tie a knot at one end. Thread the needle. Sew across the tops of the pushed-down fingers and thumb with slip stitch (see page 117), finishing with a knot. Trim the floss. You now have the bunny's head. Using embroidery floss, sew on two buttons (see page 118) for the eyes, and make a large cross stitch (see page 117) for the mouth.

2. Stuff the head with fiberfill (stuffing), carefully pushing it into the ears (see page 115). Put to one side.

3. Turn the socks inside out and lay them on the table, with the heels facing up. Take some embroidery floss, tie a knot at one end, and use running stitch (see page 116) to sew down the middle of each sock. Finish with another knot to hold the thread in place.

4. Turn the sock legs the right way out. You now have the bunny's legs. Lay them inside the opening of the bunny's head and pin in place. Cut a length of thread and tie a knot at one end. Sew running stitch across the opening, making sure that you sew through the tops of the legs. Finish with a knot and trim the thread. Remove the pins.

5. Cut out a rectangle of fabric about 12 x 6½ in. (30 x 16 cm) with pinking shears. With embroidery floss, sew the braid or bobble fringe along one long edge of the fabric. Start and finish with a few small stitches to hold the thread in place. Trim the ends of the braid or fringe to neaten them if you need to. Sew some embroidery floss across the top edge of the fabric using large running stitches. Leave the ends loose. Pull the floss slightly to gather the skirt up and tie it onto the bunny.

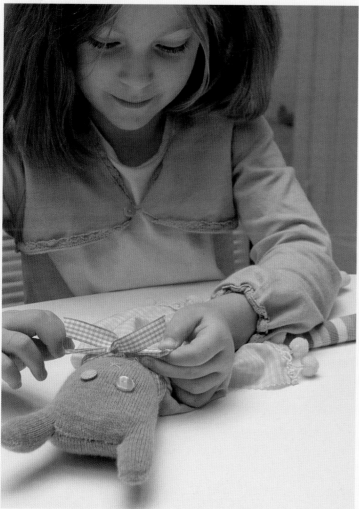

6. Finish off the bunny with a pretty ribbon tied in a bow around the bunny's neck.

Wise Old Owl

This wise old owl is a real hoot! Stitch one for yourself or give one as a gift to a friend. Sew the body and fill with fiberfill (stuffing) to make a lovely snuggly toy that is sure to be much loved. Try using your favorite colored and patterned fabrics for the front and the back of the owl to give it a really unique look.

Materials

Paper and pencil, to make the
   pattern pieces
Scissors
Fabric for the body
Pins
Needle and thread
Fiberfill (stuffing)
Felt for the feet
Scraps of fabric for the wings
White and black felt for the eyes
Black embroidery floss (thread)
   and needle
Orange felt for the beak
Orange embroidery floss
Green felt for the feathers
Green embroidery floss

1. Using the templates on page 124 and following the instructions on page 116, cut out paper patterns for the owl's body, feet, wing, eye, pupil, beak, and feathers. Fold the fabric for the body in half, pin the pattern to it, and cut out. Remove the pins and pattern.

2. Pin the two body pieces of fabric together, right sides facing. Cut a length of thread, and thread the needle. Starting with a few small stitches to hold the thread in place, sew the fabric pieces together with backstitch (see page 116) but leave the bottom edge open. Finish with a few small stitches to hold the thread in place. Trim the thread and remove the pins.

3. Turn the body the right way out and stuff with fiberfill (stuffing), pushing it well into the ears and then filling the body (see page 115). Put to one side.

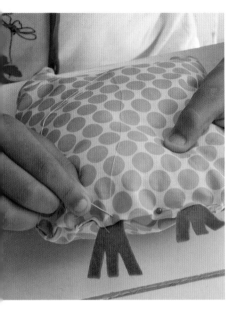

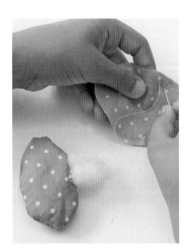

4. Fold the felt for the feet in half, pin the paper pattern to it, and cut out. Remove the pins and pattern. Turn the raw edges along the bottom of the owl's body to the inside and put the top of the feet inside the opening. Pin into position. Close the opening with backstitch, starting and finishing with a few small stitches to hold the thread in place. Trim the thread and remove the pins.

5. Fold the fabric for the wings in half, pin on the pattern from step 1, and cut out. Repeat to give you four wing pieces. Remove the pins and pattern. Pin the corresponding fabric pieces together, right sides facing. Hold the thread in place with a few small stitches, then sew the wing pieces together with backstitch. Leave a 1 in. (2.5 cm) opening in each wing. Turn the wings right way out and stuff with fiberfill. Tuck the raw edges of fabric inside the wings and close the opening using slip stitch (see page 117), starting and finishing with a few small stitches to hold the thread in place. Sew a few stitches onto the owl where one wing will go, then sew through the back of the wing. Continue sewing through both layers and finish with a few small stitches. Trim the thread. Repeat for the other wing.

6. Cut out two white circles of felt for the eyes and two slightly smaller black circles for the pupils using the pattern pieces from Step 1. Starting and finishing with a knot on the back of the eye, sew the black circles onto the white ones with black embroidery floss (thread). Use big stitches to look like eyelashes. Trim the floss.

8. Cut out three rows of feathers from the felt using the pattern piece from Step 1. Sew onto the owl with running stitch, starting and finishing with knots in the thread. Sew the bottom row on first, then overlap the middle row a little, and do the same with the top row to give a feathery look.

7. Pin the eyes onto the owl. Using the needle and thread, and starting and finishing with a few small stitches, fix the eyes in place with running stitch (see page 116). Remove the pins and trim the thread. Cut out the beak from orange felt using the pattern piece. Starting and finishing with a knot in the orange floss, sew the beak in place along the top with a few running stitches.

T-shirt Creatures

Let your creativity flow with these crazy creatures! Draw funny shapes onto old T-shirts (this is a great way of recycling T-shirts that are a little worn) and make mad faces from scraps of felt and buttons. Check with an adult before cutting up T-shirts—especially if they are not yours!

Materials

Old T-shirt
Felt-tip pen
Pins
Scissors
Needle and thread
Fiberfill (stuffing)
Scraps of felt
Buttons
Embroidery floss (thread)
    and needle
Yarn (wool)

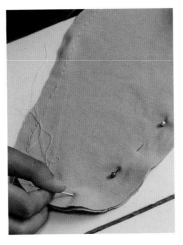

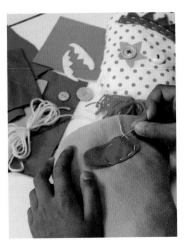

1. Turn the T-shirt inside out and lay it flat on the table. Draw the shape for your creature onto it with the felt-tip pen, making it about ¾ in. (2 cm) bigger all the way around than its final size. It can be any shape you want—the crazier, the better! Pin the layers together and cut out with scissors, making sure you cut through both layers.

2. Cut a length of thread, and thread the needle. Starting with a few small stitches to secure the end of the thread in place, sew backstitch (see page 116) all the way around your shape. Leave an opening of about 2 in. (5 cm). Remove the needle from the thread, and remove the pins.

3. Turn your shape the right way out. Fill it with fiberfill (stuffing), pushing it into any corners (see page 115). Rethread the needle and sew up the opening with backstitch. Finish with a few small stitches to hold the thread in place. Trim the thread. Next, gather together the scraps of felt and buttons you want to use to give your creature a crazy face.

4. Cut out shapes from the felt scraps and pin them in position. Cut a length of embroidery floss (thread) and thread the needle. Starting with a few stitches to fix the floss end in place, sew on the felt shapes with backstitch or running stitch (see page 116). Sew on buttons for eyes with floss (see page 118). To give your monster wild hair, wind the yarn (wool) around your hand, remove it, and tie a separate length of yarn around the middle. Sew the hair on the head with a few stitches, starting and finishing with a knot in the floss.

Variations

Instead of sewing up the heel to make a funny mouth,
you can use thread to sew on a felt mouth in running
stitch, starting and finishing with a few stitches to hold
the thread in place. If you wish, you can cut out felt
circles for the eyes to stitch onto your monster before you
sew on the buttons. Sew them onto your monster in the
same way as for the felt mouth.

Sock Monsters

Don't throw your odd socks away. Instead, transform them into monsters! Simply stuff the socks and sew funny features onto them to make a whole array of crazy creatures. This is a great project for young children, as the sewing is very simple, and little hands will have lots of fun stuffing their socks!

Materials

Sock
Scissors
Yarn (wool) and needle with
 a large eye
Fiberfill (stuffing)
Scraps of felt
Needle and thread
Buttons

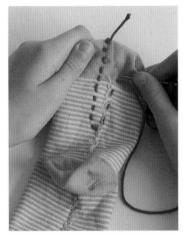

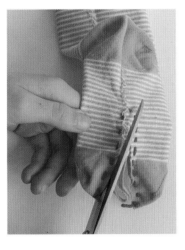

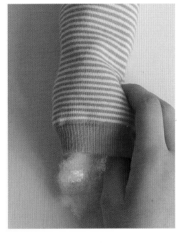

1. To make ears on your monster, turn the sock inside out. Cut a length of yarn (wool) and tie a knot at one end. Thread the large needle and sew running stitch (see page 116) from the top of the sock down 2 in. (5 cm) and then back up to the top, leaving a ½-in. (1-cm) gap between the lines of stitching. Finish with a knot and trim the yarn.

2. Cut the sock between the stitch lines, making sure you don't cut into the stitching. Turn the sock the right way out and push the ears out.

3. Fill the sock with fiberfill (stuffing) (see page 115), pushing it into the ears, or into the toe of the sock if your monster doesn't have ears. Tie a knot at one end of the yarn and sew up the end of the sock with running stitch. Finish with another knot and trim the yarn.

4. To make a funny mouth, squash the heel part of the sock slightly so that it looks like a mouth. Sew running stitch along it with yarn, starting and finishing with a knot, then trim the yarn. Next, sew buttons onto your monster to make eyes (see page 118).

Finger Puppets

Create your own farmyard with these felt finger puppets. Use the templates at the back of the book and sew pigs, horses, chickens, sheep, cows, and ducks, or use your imagination and add your own features to the basic puppet shape to make a host of different characters. Go really wild with a set of jungle animals or design your own aliens and monsters. The possibilities are endless!

Materials

Paper and pencil, to make the
   pattern pieces
Scissors
Felt in different colors
Pins
Pinking shears
Needle and thread

1. Using the template on page 122 and following the instructions on page 116, cut out a paper pattern for the main body of the puppets you wish to make. Fold a piece of felt into two, giving you two body shapes, and pin the pattern onto it. Cut out the shapes with scissors, but use pinking shears for the base of the sheep to give it a jagged edge. Remove the pins and patterns.

2. Cut out any additional paper shapes, such as a beak or mane, from the templates on page 122. If you are making a sheep, use pinking shears to cut out the face. You can either pin them onto felt or draw around them if that is easier. Cut a length of thread and tie a knot at one end. Thread the needle and use small stitches to sew the beak onto the chicken, the bill and feet onto the duck, patches on the cow, and the mane onto the horse. Finish with a knot at the back of the felt. Sew noses onto the cow, pig, and horse, and the face onto the sheep.

3. To sew eyes onto your animals, stitch French knots (see page 118). Start at the back of the felt with a knot and finish with a knot. For the sheep, sew the eyes onto the face piece. Use French knots as well to sew nostrils onto the noses of the horse, pig, and cow, and onto the face piece of the sheep.

4. For the horse, cow, or sheep, position the ears on the underside of the front of the puppet (the bit with the face on). Do the same for the chicken's comb (the red bit!). Pin the front of the puppet to the back piece of felt, making sure the ears (or comb) are in place. Working from the back, sew running stitch (see page 116) around the puppet but not across the bottom. Finish with a knot at the back and trim the thread. Remove the pins. For the pig, sew on its ears with small stiches, starting and finishing with a knot at the back.

Spoon Puppets

Spoon puppets are so easy to make that even very little hands can have a go. Draw faces onto wooden spoons or spatulas and sew clothes using simple running stitch and scraps of fabric. Make lots of characters and act out your favorite stories for friends and family.

Materials

Wooden spoon or spatula
Felt-tip pens
Scrap of fabric
Pinking shears
Scissors
Yarn (wool) and needle with
  a large eye
Scraps of yarn
Craft glue
Ribbons and buttons
  for decoration

1. Draw a face onto the back of the wooden spoon or spatula using felt-tip pens.

2. Cut out a piece of fabric measuring about 12 x 5 in. (30 x 13 cm) with pinking shears to give a jagged edge. Cut a length of yarn (wool) with scissors and thread the large needle. Sew running stitch (see page 116) across the top of the fabric, leaving about 4 in. (10 cm) of yarn at each end. Gather up the fabric by pulling the yarn, then tie it around the spoon, fastening with a knot or a bow.

3. Cut the yarn scraps into lengths to make your puppet's hair. Dab some craft glue on the top of the spoon and stick the yarn in place.

4. You can decorate your puppet in a number of ways. Tie ribbon in its hair; glue or tie ribbon around its neck; or make buttons from felt and sew them onto the fabric with a cross stitch (see page 117). You can also cut out a tie shape in fabric and glue it in place.

Chapter 2

Pretty Playthings

Mice & Toadstool

These are the kind of mice you won't mind having in your home. Create a family of them and have fun building a house for them to live in using an old box and scraps of fabric. The toadstool adds to the woodland look, and filling the stalk with dried lentils helps it to stand up.

Materials

Paper and pencil, to make the patttern pieces
Scissors
Gray and pink felt
Pins
Needle and thread
Fiberfill (stuffing)
Embroidery floss (thread) and needle
Scraps of fabric, for the dress

For the mouse

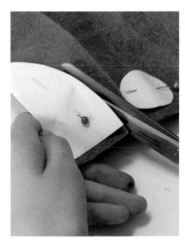    

1. Using the templates on page 123 and following the instructions on page 116, cut out a paper pattern for the mouse body, the base, and the ears. Fold the gray felt in half and pin the pattern for the mouse body onto it, placing the fold line of the pattern on the fold of the felt (see page 116). Cut out. Remove the pins and pattern. Pin the pattern for the base onto the gray felt (unfolded) and cut out. Remove the pins and pattern.

2. Cut a length of thread, and thread the needle. Fold the mouse body over and, starting and finishing with a few small stitches to hold the thread in place, sew the long edges together with slip stitch (see page 117). Leave the bottom of the felt open.

3. Starting with a few small stitches, sew the felt base onto the body with slip stitch, leaving a gap to fit in the fiberfill (stuffing).

4. Stuff small pieces of fiberfill into the mouse, pushing it well down into the nose (see page 115). When the mouse is three-quarters full add some lentils to fill the rest of the space, then continue to sew the base on and finish with a few small stitches. Trim the thread.

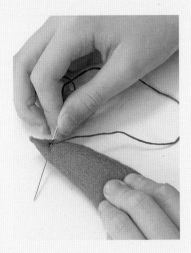

5. Cut a length of embroidery floss (thread) and tie a knot at one end. Thread the needle. Starting at the back of the mouse's head, push the needle through to the front so that it emerges in position for one of the eyes. Sew a French knot (see page 118), then stitch another for the second eye, taking the floss through to the back of the head. Finish with a small knot. Trim the floss.

6. Pin the pattern for the ears onto the pink felt. Cut out. Remove the pins and pattern. Sew a few small stitches on the back of the head using the needle and thread. Stitch through the ears and then back through the mouse. Repeat this a few times to hold the ears in place and finish with a few small stitches. Trim the thread.

7. To make the dress, cut out a little piece of fabric measuring about 5 x 1½ in. (13 x 4 cm). With embroidery floss, stitch along one of the longer sides using running stitch (see page 116). Leave both ends of the floss free. Unthread the needle and tie the dress onto the mouse, trimming the ends of the floss if they are too long.

For the toadstool

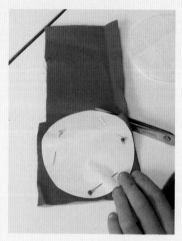

Materials

EXTRAS FOR THE TOADSTOOL
Red and white felt
Small spoon
Dried lentils

1. Using the templates on page 126 and following the instructions, cut out a paper pattern for the toadstool top, the stalk, and the base. Pin the pattern for the toadstool top onto a piece of red felt and cut out. Then pin it to a piece of white felt and cut that out, too. Pin the stalk and base patterns onto white felt and cut out one of each. Remove all the pins and patterns.

2. Cut out some small circles from white felt—don't worry about them being perfect circles. Arrange them on the red felt toadstool top. Starting and finishing with a few small stitches on the underside of the red felt, use the needle and thread to sew the felt dots in place with running stitch or slip stitch. Finish with a few small stitches, and trim the thread.

Tip

When making your mouse family, dress the boys in a bowtie made from a small bow of ribbon, stitched at the neck, and sew one or two small buttons onto the front to look like a shirt. Why not make some larger mice by photocopying the templates on page 123 to the size that you would like and following the instructions above.

3. Pin the red spotty top to the white felt toadstool top. Starting with a few small stitches, slipstitch them together around the edge using the needle and thread. Leave a small opening of about 1¼ in. (3 cm) and stuff with fiberfill. Stitch up the opening and finish with a few small stitches. Trim the thread and remove the pins.

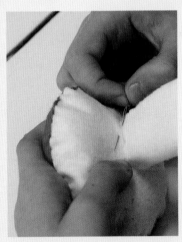

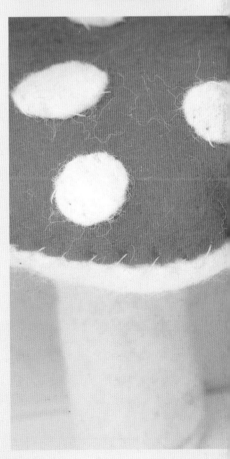

4. Take the felt stalk piece and fold it in half lengthwise. Starting and finishing with a few small stitches, sew the two long edges together with slip stitch. Keep the stitches quite close together so that the dried lentils (see Step 6) can't escape.

5. Push the stalk out so that it looks like a tube. Starting and finishing with a few small stitches, sew one end to the middle of the underside of the toadstool top using slip stitch. Trim the thread.

6. Push some fiberfill inside the stalk up to around halfway. Start to stitch the base onto the open end of the stalk with slip stitch. Halfway around, spoon dried lentils into the stalk until it is full. Continue to sew the base onto the stalk, finishing with a few small stitches. Trim the thread.

Rag Dolls

These lovely ladies are quite easy to make but take a little time, so are perhaps more suited to the slightly older stitcher. Choose felt in skin tones and sew with matching embroidery floss to make an adorable doll that will become a favorite playmate for years to come. You can then give your doll a makeover with the pretty clothes you will find on page 34.

Materials

Paper and pencil, to make the pattern pieces
Scissors
Felt for the body, arms, and legs
Pins
Embroidery floss (thread) and needle
Fiberfill (stuffing)
Felt in a different color for the hair
Scraps of felt for the eyes and mouth
Craft glue

 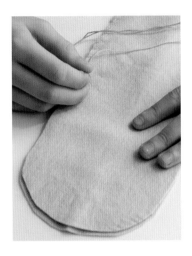 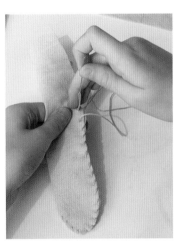 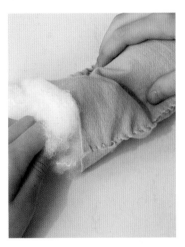

1. Using the templates on page 125 and following the instructions on page 116, cut out paper patterns for the body, an arm, and a leg, and the front and back of the hair. Put the patterns for the hair to one side. Fold the felt for the body, arms, and legs. Lay the patterns on top of the felt, making sure that a long edge of the arm and leg patterns are positioned on the fold (see page 116), then pin in place. Cut them out. You will need two body pieces, two arm pieces, and two leg pieces. Remove the pins and patterns.

2. Pin the two body pieces together. Cut a length of embroidery floss (thread) and tie a knot at one end. Thread the needle. Use slip stitch (see page 117) to sew all the way around the edge but leaving the bottom edge open. Finish with a knot on the same side as you started and trim the floss. Remove the pins. Put to one side.

3. Take a leg piece and fold it in half lengthwise. Pin to hold in place. Tie a knot at one end of the embroidery floss and slipstitch around the foot and down the leg, leaving the top open. Finish with a knot on the same side. Remove the pins. Sew both legs in this way, then do the same for both arms.

4. Stuff the body, arms, and legs, pushing the fiberfill (stuffing) down to the ends (see page 115).

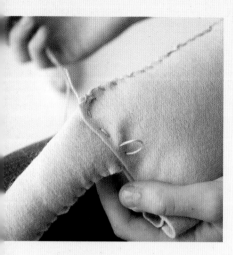
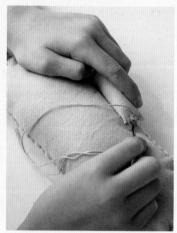
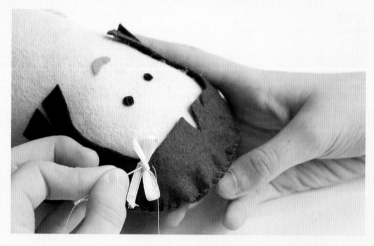

5. Push the tops of the legs inside the bottom edge of the body and pin in place. Tie a knot at one end of the floss and, working from the back of the doll, sew running stitch (see page 116) all the way across, finishing with a knot on the same side as you started. Remove the pins.

6. Take the arms and slipstitch across the top, with the seam in the middle. Start and finish with a knot in the floss. Slip-stitch the arms in place on the body, starting and finishing with a knot.

7. Cut out a front and back for the hair from felt, using the patterns from Step 1. Starting and finishing with knots in the floss, slipstitch the two pieces together. Place on the head and hold in place with a few small stitches in the top of the head.

Next, cut out small dots for eyes and a smiley mouth from felt and sew or glue them onto the doll's face. Add a bow or pretty flower if you like, either sewing in place or using a small dab of glue.

Tip

When stuffing the body, arms, and legs, don't use too much fiberfill (stuffing) as it can make the seams split. Use small pieces of fiberfill and loosely fill the felt shapes, leaving a little room at the bottom of the body and at the tops of the arms and legs, so that you will be able to stitch them closed more easily.

Doll's Clothes

Once you have sewn your own doll, you will need to dress her. Make a pretty skirt, top, and a stylish coat with a cute pair of shoes to finish the look. You can also use fabric scraps to stitch a little bag and head scarf, which will no doubt delight your dollies.

Materials

Fabric for the top
Pinking shears
Pins
Needle and thread
Scissors
Braid or rickrack (optional)
Small piece of Velcro
Safety pin
Fabric for the skirt
Ribbon for the skirt, about 12 in. (30 cm) long
Paper and pencil, to make the pattern pieces for the coat and shoes
Felt for the coat
Felt for the shoes
2 buttons
Small scissors

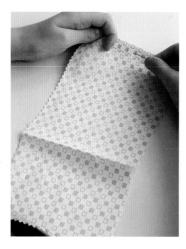

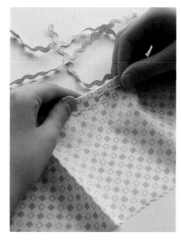

1. To make the top, cut out a rectangle of fabric measuring 5 x 10¼ in. (13 x 26 cm) with pinking shears. Fold over the two short edges by about ½ in. (1 cm) to the wrong side (see page 115). Pin into place. Thread the needle and sew running stitch (see page 116) along them, starting and finishing with a few small stitches to hold the sewing in place. Trim the thread. Remove the pins.

2. Fold over the top edge of the fabric to the wrong side. Pin into place and sew running stitch along it in the same way. If you wish, sew braid or rickrack along it using running stitch. Start and finish with a few small stitches. Trim the thread and remove the pins.

3. Separate the Velcro and sew one piece to the right side of the rectangle (in the top left-hand corner) and the other piece to the wrong side of the rectangle (in the top right-hand corner), starting and finishing with a knot on the wrong side. Wrap the top around the doll and fasten at the back with the Velcro.

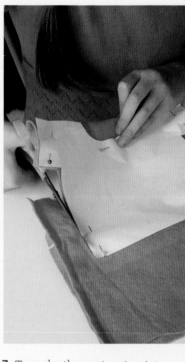

5. Fold over the top edge of the fabric by about ¾ in. (2 cm) and sew running stitch along it as in Step 2.

6. Fasten the safety pin through one end of the ribbon. Thread the safety pin and ribbon through the top of the rectangle between the stitches and the fold. Remove the safety pin. Tie the ribbon around the doll's waist and fasten with a bow at the back.

7. To make the coat, cut out a paper pattern using the template on page 125 and following the instructions on page 116. Fold the felt in half. Pin the pattern onto the felt, positioning the shoulders along the fold (see page 116). This will give you the front and back of the coat, joined at the shoulders. Cut out with scissors. Remove the pins and pattern. Cut down the middle of the front of the coat, as shown on the template.

4. To make the skirt, cut out a rectangle of fabric measuring 21 x 7½ in. (54 x 19 cm) with pinking shears. Fold over the two short edges to the wrong side by about ½ in. (1 cm) and sew running stitch along them as in Step 1.

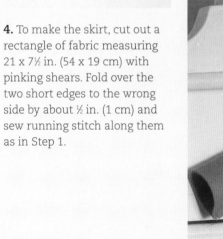

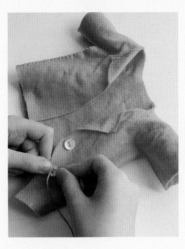
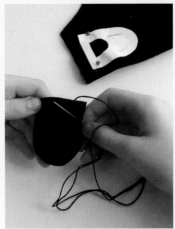

8. Fold the coat along the shoulders and pin together the arms and also the sides. Thread the needle and slipstitch (see page 117) together, starting and finishing with a few small stitches. Trim the thread. Remove the pins.

9. Fold back a little of the felt around the neck to make a collar. Sew a few small stitches in the corner of the collar to hold it in place. Trim the thread. Sew on buttons for decoration (see page 118).

10. To make the shoes, cut out a paper pattern using the templates on page 125. Pin them to the felt and cut out, using small scissors to cut out the inset in the top of the shoe. You will need to cut out two pieces of felt for the tops of the shoes and two pieces for the bottoms. Remove the pins and pattern. Pin each top piece of felt to a bottom piece and slipstitch around the edges, leaving the tops open. Start and finish with a few small stitches to hold the thread in place. Trim the thread. Remove the pins. Now the clothes are ready to put on your doll!

Tip

Why not cut a triangle of fabric large enough to fit around your doll's head to make a lovely headscarf. To make a shoulder bag cut a piece of fabric measuring 4 x 2½ in. (10 x 6 cm). Fold in half lengthways and sew along either side with running stitch. Finish with a 9 in. (23cm) length of ribbon stitched onto either side to make the handle. Sew beads and sequins onto the bag and make a pair of matching shoes to complete the outfit.

Doll's Bedding

Keep your dolls and teddies cozy with this lovely blanket and pillow set. Choose two fabrics or for a simpler version use just one piece for the front instead of adding a border, then miss out the rickrack trim. Use nice, soft fiberfill (stuffing) so that your toys are sure to get a good nights sleep, or if you haven't got any to hand cut up old T-shirts into strips and use that instead.

Materials

Pencil
2 pieces of fabric
Ruler
Scissors
Pins
Needle and thread
Rickrack or ribbon
Batting (wadding)
Fiberfill (stuffing)

1. To make a bed cover, draw a 16½ x 14 in. (42 x 36 cm) rectangle on a piece of fabric with a pencil and ruler, and another 16½ x 4¾ in. (42 x 12 cm) rectangle on a second bit of fabric. Cut out. With right sides together, pin the border piece to the main piece. Cut a length of thread, and thread the needle. Starting and finishing with a few small stitches to hold the thread in place, sew backstitch (see page 116) to join the sides together. Trim the thread and remove the pins.

2. Open the top flap out and lay the fabric flat on the table, right side up. Cut a length of rickrack or ribbon, about 17 in. (43 cm) long, and pin along the seam (the join of the fabrics). Starting and finishing with a few small stitches, sew the rickrack in place with running stitch (see page 116). Trim the thread and remove pins.

3. Use the pencil and ruler to draw a rectangle measuring 17¾ x 16½ in. (46 x 42 cm) on the same fabric used for the border piece. Cut out. Pin this to the rectangle with the rickrack, right sides together. Starting and finishing with a few small stitches, sew them together with backstitch, sewing along both sides and across the top. Leave the bottom open. Trim the thread and remove the pins.

4. Turn the cover the right way out. Using a pencil and ruler, draw a rectangle measuring 17¼ x 16 in. (44 x 40 cm) on the batting (wadding). Cut out. Put the batting inside the cover, making sure the corners of the batting are properly in place. Fold the raw bottom edges of the fabric to the inside by ½ in. (1 cm) and pin both edges together. Slipstitch (see page 117) across this edge, starting and finishing with a few small stitches. Remove the pins and trim the thread.

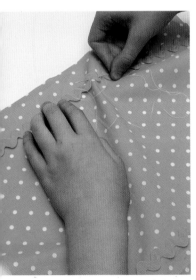

5. To make the pillow, use the pencil and ruler to draw a rectangle measuring 13 x 10 in. (33 x 25 cm) on the same fabric as the smaller rectangle in Step 1. Cut two lengths of rickrack, just over 10 in. (25 cm) each, and pin them onto the right side along the two short sides of the fabric, about 2 in. (5 cm) in from either edge. Starting and finishing with a few small stitches, sew the rickrack in place with running stitch. Trim the thread and remove the pins.

6. Fold the fabric in half, right sides together, and pin. Starting and finishing with a few small stitches, sew around the fabric using backstitch, leaving a small opening of about 2 in. (5 cm). Remove the needle from the thread and remove the pins. Turn the fabric the right way out and fill with fiberfill (stuffing) (see page 115). Rethread the needle and slipstitch the opening closed, finishing with a few small stitches. Trim the thread.

Fabric Tea Set

Any one for tea? This is a very simple project and is as much fun to make as it is to play with. Stitch a few teacups, invite your friends (or your teddies!) round, and have yourselves the perfect tea party. Make the teapot and cups in the same fabric or use scraps of different fabrics for a delightfully individual set.

Materials

Pencil
Ruler
Fabric
Scissors
Paper, to make the pattern pieces
Pins
Needle and thread
Fiberfill (stuffing)
Compass
White and pale brown felt
Batting (wadding)
Embroidery floss (thread) and a needle

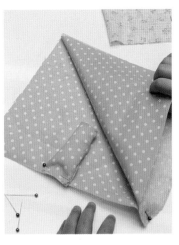

1. For the teapot, use the pencil and ruler to draw a 15¾ x 9 in. (40 x 23 cm) rectangle on a piece of paper. Cut out. Pin the pattern to a piece of fabric and cut out. Remove the pins and pattern. For the teacup, repeat the above instructions but use a rectangle measuring 9 x 4¼ in. (23 x 11 cm) for the pattern instead.

2. Using the template on page 126 and following the instructions on page 116, cut out a paper pattern for the spout. Fold a piece of fabric in half and pin the spout pattern along the fold (see page 116). Cut out. Remove the pins and pattern. Cut a length of thread, and thread the needle. Fold the spout shape over, right sides together, and, starting and finishing with a few small stitches, use backstitch (see page 116) to sew along the short end and the raw long side. Trim the thread.

3. Take the fabric rectangle for the teapot and lay it flat on the table, right side up. Pin the spout to the teapot halfway down one short side, matching up the raw edges. Fold the fabric rectangle over and pin the short edges together. Sew a few small stitches at one end and use backstitch to join the short sides together, stitching through the spout as you go. Finish with a few small stitches. Trim the thread. Remove the pins. Stitch the short edges of the teacup fabric together in the same way, but missing out the spout.

4. Turn the teapot and teacup the right way out. Starting with a few small stitches, sew running stitch (see page 116) around one end of both pieces. Pull the thread and gather up the fabric and finish with a few small stitches.

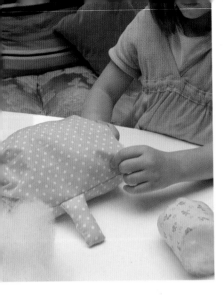

5. Push fiberfill (stuffing) inside the teapot until it is a nice round shape. Gather up the fabric at the open end in the same way as in Step 4. Do the same with the teacup.

6. Set the compass to 1¾ in. (4.5 cm) wide and draw a circle on paper. This is for the teapot lid. Reset the compass to a width of 1¼ in. (3 cm), and draw another circle for the base of the teapot. Cut these out and pin them onto a piece of white felt. Cut out. Remove the pins and patterns. Starting and finishing with a few small stitches, sew the larger circle onto the top of the teapot and the smaller circle to the bottom using running stitch. Trim the thread. Use the smaller paper circle to cut out one pale brown felt circle and one white circle. Starting and finishing with a few small stitches, use running stitch to sew the brown circle onto the top and the white circle onto the bottom of the teacup.

7. To make the teapot handle, cut out a piece of fabric measuring 2¼ x 7 in. (6 x 18 cm) and a piece of batting (wadding) measuring 1¼ x 6 in. (3 x 15 cm). Lay the batting in the middle of the fabric and fold in the edges and ends of the fabric. Fold the whole thing in half lengthwise and pin together. Starting and finishing with a few small stitches, sew running stitch through all the layers. Using a few stitches, sew the handle in place on the teapot, making sure that it is securely held in place. Trim the thread. Remove the pins. For the teacup handle, follow the above instructions but use fabric measuring 4 x 2 in. (10 x 5 cm) and batting 2¾ x ¾ in. (7 x 2 cm).

8. To make the knob on the teapot lid, set the compass to 1¾ in. (4.5 cm) and draw a circle on paper. Cut out. Pin the paper circle to a piece of fabric and cut out. Remove the pins and paper. Starting with a few small stitches, sew running stitch all the way around it. Pull the thread and gather the fabric, putting a little piece of fiberfill in the middle of it. Secure the stitching with a few small stitches and trim the thread. Sew this to the top of the teapot with a few small stitches.

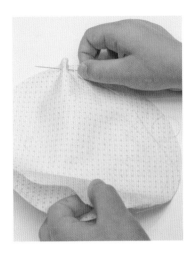  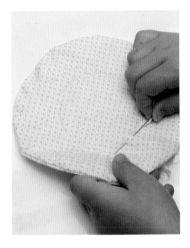 

9. To make the saucer, set the compass to 3¼ in. (8 cm) and draw a circle on paper. Cut out. Fold a piece of fabric in two and pin the circle to it. Cut out. Remove the pins and paper. Starting with a few small stitches, use backstitch to sew the fabric circles together, with right sides facing. Leave a small gap of about 2 in. (5 cm).

10. Remove the thread from the needle. Turn the fabric circle the right way out. Set the compass to 2¾ in. (7 cm) and draw a circle on paper. Pin the paper circle to a piece of batting and cut out. Remove the pins. Push the circle of batting inside the saucer, making sure that it lies flat. Rethread the needle and sew up the opening, finishing with a few stitches.

11. Cut a length of embroidery floss (thread) and tie a knot at one end. Thread the needle. Starting on the underside of the saucer, sew a circle of running stitch in the center as the indent for the teacup. Finish with a knot on the same side as the first one and trim the floss.

12. Using the templates on page 126 and following the instructions, cut out a paper pattern for the bowl of the spoon and for the handle. Fold a piece of felt in half and pin the pattern for the bowl of the spoon onto it. Cut out. Remove the pins and pattern. Pin the two felt shapes together. Pin the pattern for the handle to a piece of fabric and cut out. Remove the pins and pattern. Fold over the edges of the handle fabric and then fold that over the bowl of the spoon fabric. Pin the bowl of the spoon and the handle together. Starting with a knot in the embroidery floss on the underside of the spoon, stitch them together with running stitch. Finish with a knot on the same side. Trim the floss and remove the pins. Pour yourself a cup of tea!

Felt Cupcakes

These yummy cakes look good enough to eat. Choose felt in pretty pastel colors and decorate with embroidery floss (thread) or, for scrumptious chocolate cakes, use brown felt, adding some rickrack trim for a delicious cream filling!

Materials

Paper and pencil, to make the pattern pieces
Scissors
Pins
Selection of felt in browns, pastel shades, and a bright color for the cherry
Embroidery floss (thread) in similar colors and a needle
Fiberfill (stuffing)

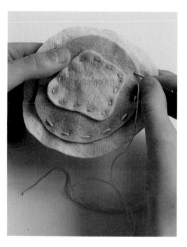

1. Using the templates on page 121 and following the instructions on page 116, cut out the pattern pieces for the cupcake top, the cupcake bottom, the frosting (icing), and the cherry. Pin the large circle onto felt in a pastel shade, the medium-sized circle onto brown or beige felt, and the frosting shape onto white or pastel-colored felt. Cut out. Remove the pins and patterns.

2. Pin the frosting shape onto the cupcake top shape. Cut a length of embroidery floss (thread) and tie a knot at one end. Thread the needle. Starting from the back of the felt, sew running stitch (see page 116) all the way around the frosting to hold the two pieces together. Finish with another knot on the back of the felt. Remove the pins.

3. Put these joined pieces of felt in the middle of the largest felt circle. Knot the floss and sew running stitch around the edge of the cupcake top, as you did in Step 2, making the stitches quite big. Leave a gap of about 1 in. (2.5 cm) for the fiberfill (stuffing).

4. Take small pieces of the fiberfill and carefully push them inside the cupcake through the gap (see page 115). Add enough to make the cupcake nicely rounded. When you have finished stuffing the cupcake, continue the running stitch to close the gap and finish with a knot on the underside.

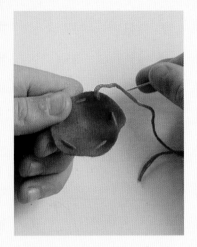

5. Pin the paper pattern for the cherry to the brightly colored felt. Cut out. Remove the pins and pattern. Cut a length of floss, tie a knot at one end, and thread the needle. Sew running stitch around the outside of the felt.

6. Pull the floss slightly to gather the cherry up. Stuff it with a small piece of fiberfill. Pull the floss a little more and sew a few stitches to hold it in place. Don't cut the floss. Stitch the cherry in place using a few small stitches and finish with a knot or several little stitches to hold it in place. Trim the floss.

Variation

Try using the templates on page 121 to make a delicious frosted bun. Small stitches made with different colored floss will give the bun sprinkles, or sew a length of rickrack around the cake using running stitch for a cream filling.

Chapter 3

Fashion Fun

Embroidered Jeans

Personalize your plain clothes with some simple embroidery stitches to create something that will really get you noticed. Chain stitches form cute lazy daisies when grouped together with sequins and beads, adding a glittery finishing touch. Make up your own designs and use them to decorate jackets and bags as well.

Materials

Pair of jeans
Felt-tip or air-soluble pen
Scissors
Embroidery floss (thread) in pretty colors, including green for the leaves, and a needle
Scissors
Needle and thread
Sequins
Bugle beads

1. Mark the position of the flowers at the bottom of your jeans with either a felt-tip or an air-soluble pen (see page 115). Keep the marks as small as you can. Cut a length of embroidery floss (thread) and tie a knot at one end. Working from the inside of one of the legs, sew five chain stitches (see page 117) in a flower shape. Finish with a knot inside the leg and trim the floss. Repeat for the rest of the flower—we have sewn three flowers in three different colors.

2. Cut a length of green embroidery floss and tie a knot at one end. Thread the floss. Working from the inside of the leg, sew three separate chain stitches to look like leaves around the flowers. Finish with a knot inside the leg and trim the floss.

3. To add sequins, cut a length of thread, and thread the needle at one end. Starting from inside the leg, sew a few small stitches close to a flower to fix the thread in place. Bring the needle up through the denim in the center of the flower, push it through the sequin hole, then back through the denim at the sequin edge. Bring the needle back through the sequin again and back down through the denim on the other side. Sew on more sequins in the same way. Finish with a few small stitches on the inside of the jeans. Trim the thread.

4. Sew on bugle beads in between the flower petals in the same way as the sequins, stitching just once to hold them in place. Stitch back through the jeans and finish with a few small stitches. Trim the thread. You can, if you wish, repeat the above steps on the other leg of your jeans.

Barrettes

These gorgeous hair barrettes are very quick to make and are a great way of using up scraps of felt left over from other projects. Blanket stitch is used to sew around the shape—it is a good idea to practice this stitch on scrap felt. It looks complicated but is actually quite easy once you get the hang of it.

Materials

Paper and pencil, to make the pattern pieces
Scissors
Felt
Pins
Embroidery floss (thread) and needle
Fiberfill (stuffing)
Button
Metal barrettes (hair slides)

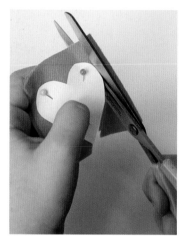

1. Using the templates on page 119 and following the instructions on page 116, cut out a circle or heart shape from paper. Fold the felt and pin the pattern onto it. Cut out the felt. This will give you two shapes. Remove the pins and pattern. Pin the shapes together.

2. Cut a length of embroidery floss (thread) and tie a knot at one end. Thread the needle. Sew blanket stitch around the felt (see page 117), leaving a small opening.

3. Stuff the shape with little pieces of fiberfill (stuffing).

4. Continue using blanket stitch to close the opening and finish with a knot at the back of the shape. Trim the floss.

5. Sew a button onto the front of the shape, following the instructions on page 118.

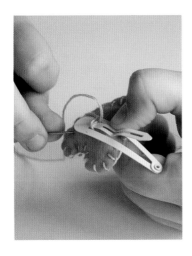

6. Tie a knot at one end of the embroidery floss. Make a stitch through the back of the shape and then stitch through the barrette (hair slide). Continue to stitch through the back of the shape and the barrette so that they are firmly held together. Finish with a knot and trim the floss.

Variation

Instead of using the heart template in Step 1, you can draw two circles on paper with a pencil and compass, one measuring 5½ in. (14 cm) in diameter, the other 3¼ in. (8 cm), and cut them out to make a pattern. You then follow the instructions as opposite.

Appliqué T-shirt

Appliqué is a simple but very effective sewing technique. It involves cutting out shapes from fabric and using them to decorate a backing fabric. Here it is used to decorate a plain T-shirt using hearts or circles, with running stitch edging the shapes. Bondaweb is used to stop the fabric fraying, which is important if you are appliquéing something that will be washed regularly.

Materials

Paper and pencil, to make the pattern pieces
Scissors
2 pieces of patterned fabric
Iron
Wonder-Under (Bondaweb)
Pencil
Plain T-shirt
Embroidery floss (thread) in different colors and needle

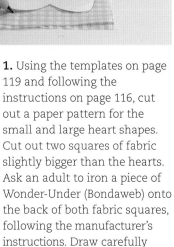

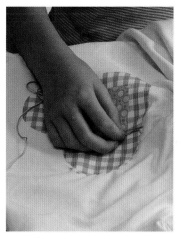

1. Using the templates on page 119 and following the instructions on page 116, cut out a paper pattern for the small and large heart shapes. Cut out two squares of fabric slightly bigger than the hearts. Ask an adult to iron a piece of Wonder-Under (Bondaweb) onto the back of both fabric squares, following the manufacturer's instructions. Draw carefully around each heart with a pencil on the back of these squares.

2. Cut out the fabric hearts with a pair of scissors, taking care to achieve a smooth finish around the edges.

3. Ask an adult to help you iron the T-shirt so that there are no creases in it. Peel off the backing paper from the Wonder-Under. Lay the fabric hearts on the front of the T-shirt, centering the small one over the larger one. Place a damp cloth over the top and, with an adult's help, press the T-shirt with an iron. Remove the cloth.

4. Cut a length of embroidery floss (thread) and tie a knot at one end. Thread the needle. Starting from the inside of the T-shirt, use running stitch (see page 116) to decorate around the heart, finishing with a knot on the inside of the T-shirt. Trim the floss. For extra decoration, you could sew a line of running stitch around the inner heart.

Flower Hair Ties

Brighten up your braids or ponytail with these cute hair decorations. Made of felt flowers sewn onto hair ties, clips, or bands in your favorite colors, with a button in the center, they are a pretty finishing touch to any outfit.

Materials

Paper and pencil, to make the pattern pieces
Scissors
Pins
Felt in 2 colors for the flower and in green for the leaves
Embroidery floss (thread) and needle
Button
Elastic hair tie

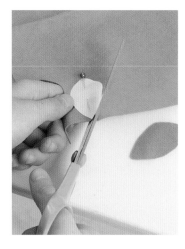

1. Using the template on page 126 and following the instructions on page 116, cut out a paper pattern for a flower and another for a leaf. Pin the flower shape onto one of the pieces of felt and cut out. Remove the pins and pattern. Repeat on the second piece of felt, so that you have two flower shapes.

2. Pin the leaf pattern to the green felt. Cut out. Remove the pins and pattern. Repeat, to give you two leaf shapes.

3. Put the two flower shapes on top of each other, and place the leaf shapes behind them. Cut a length of embroidery floss (thread). Thread the needle and tie a knot at one end. From the back, stitch through the two leaves (near their ends) and through the center of the flowers. Pull the floss so that the knot is in place.

4. Take the button and push the needle through one of the buttonholes. Pull the button along the floss so that it sits in the middle of the flower.

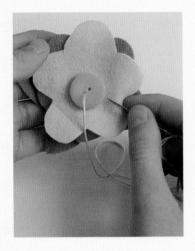

5. Stitch back through the other hole in the button and push the needle carefully though all the layers of felt. Repeat this stitch through the felt and the button again to hold it firmly in place. If you are using a button with four holes, then make two stitches through the other holes as well.

6. Place the hair tie on the back of the flower and leaves, and make a few stitches, starting and finishing with a knot to hold it in place. Trim the floss. Make another decorative hair tie in the same way if you would like a pair.

Yo-yo Necklace

The great thing about this pretty necklace is that no one will be able to tell that it is made from scraps of fabric and it makes a great gift that everyone is sure to love. Try making bracelets using a row of small gathered yo-yos or sew safety pins onto the back of individual yo-yos to make pretty brooches.

Materials

Pencil and compass
Paper
Scissors
Pins
Scraps of fabric
Needle and thread
Buttons
Ribbon

1. Set the compass to 2 in. (5 cm) wide and draw a circle on paper. Reset the compass to a width of 1½ in. (4 cm) and draw a second circle. Cut out. Pin these patterns to the fabric scraps and cut out. Remove the pins and patterns.

2. Cut a length of thread, and thread the needle. Sew a few small stitches near the edge of one of the fabric circles, then sew running stitch (see page 116) all the way around the circle. Pull the thread at the end to gather up the fabric, making the yo-yo. Finish with a few small stitches, cut the thread, then flatten the yo-yo with your hand. Make several yo-yos in this way. We used three large circles and two smaller ones.

3. Sew the three larger yo-yos together in a line with a few small stitches through the edges of each of them. Sew a small yo-yo to each end to form a slight curve.

4. Sew a button onto the middle of each yo-yo (see page 118).

5. Cut two lengths of ribbon about 8 in. (20 cm) long. Sew a few small stitches through the edge of an outer (small) yo-yo, then stitch one end of a ribbon to it. Secure the ribbon in place with some more stitches, then trim the thread. Repeat with the second length of ribbon, sewing it to the other outer yo-yo. To wear the necklace, simply tie the ribbons in a bow at the back of your neck.

Chapter 4

Bags, Books & Bedroom Bits 'n' Pieces

Tote Bag

Every girl needs a cute bag and what could be better than creating one yourself from your favorite materials? Rectangles of fabric are joined using backstitch to make the perfect carrier for all your bits and pieces. Decorate with a ribbon bow or why not make a fabric yo-yo following the instructions for the necklace on page 56 and stitch it onto the bag to add a stylish touch.

Materials

Pencil
Ruler
Paper
Scissors
2 pieces of fabric
Pins
Needle and thread
Wide ribbon for the handles, about 24 in. (60 cm) long
Narrow ribbon for the bow

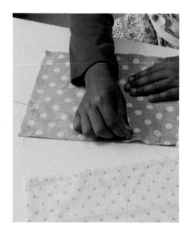

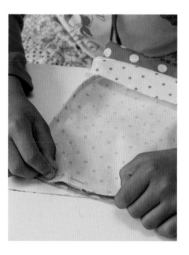

1. Using the pencil and ruler, draw a rectangle measuring 8½ x 10 in. (22 x 25 cm) onto paper. Cut out. Fold one of the pieces of fabric in half and pin the pattern to it. Cut out. Remove the pins and pattern. This will give you two rectangles. Repeat this using the second piece of fabric. Decide which fabric you would like for the outside of the bag and which for the lining.

2. Pin the two rectangles for the outside of the bag together, right sides facing. Cut a length of thread, and thread the needle. Start and finish with small stitches to fix the thread in place and use backstitch (see page 116) to sew up both long sides and the bottom. Trim the thread. Remove the pins. Take the lining rectangles and pin together, right sides facing. Starting and finishing with a few small stitches to secure the thread, sew backstitch along the long sides, leaving the two short sides open. Trim the thread and remove the pins.

3. Turn the outside of the bag the right way out. Cut the length of ribbon in half, so each piece is 12 in. (30 cm) long. Line up one ribbon end with the raw edge of the bag, placing it about 2¼ in. (6 cm) from one side. Pin ribbon in position, ensuring you go through only one layer of fabric. Thread the needle and sew the ribbon in place loosely with a few small stitches. Trim thread and remove pins. Repeat with the other end of the ribbon, positioning it the same distance from the facing side. Do the same to fix the second ribbon to the other side of the bag.

4. With the lining still inside out, slip it over the outside of the bag. Pin the top edges of the lining and bag together. Starting and finishing with a few small stitches, use backstitch to sew around the top edge, stitching the lining to the bag. Trim the thread and remove the pins.

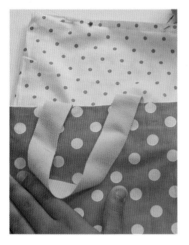

5. Turn the lining the right way out. Fold under the raw edges of the lining by about ½ in. (1 cm) and pin both sides together. Starting and finishing with a few small stitches, slipstitch across the lining. Trim the thread and remove the pins. Push the lining inside the bag.

6. Tie a piece of ribbon into a bow. Sew a few small stitches onto the bag at the base of one of the handles and then sew through the back of the bow. Continue to sew through the bag and the ribbon to hold it in place. Finish with a few small stitches on the inside of the bag. Trim the thread.

Bag Decoration

Jazz up a plain bag with these great felt decorations. Cut circles of felt and play around with the color combinations, then stitch them together using running stitch and blanket stitch. To turn them into brooches, simply stitch a safety pin on the back and attach to clothing or give as gifts.

Materials

Paper and pencil, to make the pattern pieces
Scissors
Felt in 3 contrasting colors
Pins
Embroidery floss (thread) and needle
Needle and thread

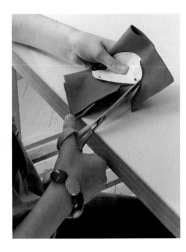

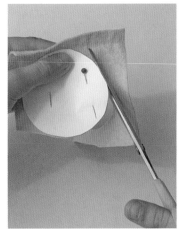

1. Using the templates on page 120 and following the instructions on page 116, make a paper pattern for each of the three circles. Fold one piece of felt in half and pin the largest pattern onto it. Cut out, making sure you cut through both layers. Remove the pins and pattern.

2. Pin the two felt circles together. Sew blanket stitch (see page 117) with embroidery floss (thread) all the way around to join the two circles together. Finish with a few small stitches through the back piece of felt for security. Remove the pins.

3. Pin the middle-sized pattern onto different-colored felt and cut out (you need only one layer this time). Remove the pins and pattern.

4. With scissors, make little snips all the way around the felt, cutting out small triangles.

Tip

Make several more circles in the same way in different sizes and colors, then attach them to your bag for a stylish and individual look. You can also vary the number of snips you put in the centre circle, or even use different shapes for the felt pieces to customize your bag.

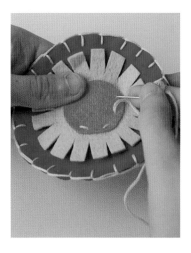

5. Pin the smallest paper pattern onto the third piece of felt and cut out (again, you need only one layer of felt). Remove the pins and pattern. Place the smallest felt circle in the middle of the circle next up in size. Then place these two circles in the middle of the largest one. Pin into position. Sew running stitch (see page 116) with floss around the edge of the smallest circle through all the layers, starting and finishing with a knot on the back. Remove the pins. Cut a length of thread and thread the

needle. Working from the inside of your bag, sew a few securing stitches in the position where you want the felt decoration to be. Then sew through the back of the decoration a few times so that there are no visible stitches but the decoration is still held firmly in place. Finish with a knot on the inside of the bag and trim the thread.

Drawstring Bags

These little bags are very easy to make and perfect for storing toys, jewelry, and little treasures. You can make them in any size—simply cut out a rectangle of fabric twice the width of the bag that you want plus ¾ in. (2cm), and add 2 in. (5cm) to the height, then follow the instructions below. Make the bags as gifts for family and friends, filling them with sweets, pretty shells, or beads.

Materials

Fabric
Pinking shears
Ruler
Pencil
Scissors
Needle and thread
Safety pin
Ribbon
Scraps of felt
Embroidery floss (thread)
  and needle

  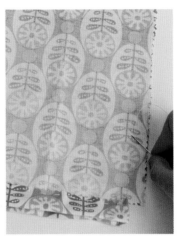 

1. Take the fabric and make a rectangle measuring 14 x 10 in. (34 x 24 cm), drawing lines with the pencil. Cut out the rectangle with pinking shears, which will help to stop the fabric fraying. Lay the rectangle of fabric on the table, wrong side facing up and with a short edge at the top, and measure 1½ in. (4 cm) down from both top corners. Using scissors, make a snip about ⅜ in. (1 cm) long on each side at this point.

2. Fold over the flap of fabric above the snip to the wrong side (see page 115) by ½ in. (1 cm) and pin it in place. Cut a length of thread and sew running stitch (see page 116) along the right-hand corner to hold the fabric in place, starting and finishing with a few small stitches. Repeat on the left-hand corner. Remove the pins.

3. Fold the top edge of the fabric rectangle over to the wrong side by ½ in. (1.5 cm) and pin in place. Sew running stitch along it, starting and finishing with a few small stitches. Remove the pins. Fold the fabric in half down its length with right sides together (see page 115) and line up the edges. Pin together, then sew running stitch down the side and along the bottom to form a bag. Start and finish with a few small stitches as before. Turn the bag the right way out.

4. Cut a piece of ribbon about 18 in. (45 cm) long. Fasten the safety pin through one end of it and pass it through the channel at the top of the bag until it comes out of the other side. Remove the safety pin.

5. Cut out two small circles or squares of felt. Cut a length of embroidery floss (thread) and tie a knot at one end. Stitch through both ends of the ribbon and then sew a felt circle on each side of the ribbon, with a small running stitch around the edge. Finish with a few small stitches or a knot in the floss. Trim the floss.

Tip

To make your bag as strong as possible, keep your stitches as small and neat as you can to stop the seams coming apart. For heavier items, like marbles, sew two rows of backstitch over each other to prevent the bag from splitting. Why not decorate your bags by sewing felt shapes onto them. Cut out the letters for your name or make patterns with buttons and beads to add the finishing touch.

Cat Bag

This handy little bag is a nice and simple project to make that will be much admired by everyone who sees it. Made from fleece fabric, it uses very simple stitches and is a good starter project. Why not design your own bag. You could choose a dog, mouse, or rabbit, adding whiskers and floppy ears to make a funny face.

Materials

Paper and pencil, to make the pattern pieces
Scissors
Fleece fabric
Pins
Embroidery floss (thread) in 2 colors and needle
Felt for the nose
Scrap of fabric for the ears
2 buttons
Ribbon for the handle
Ribbon for the bow

 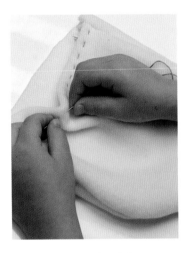 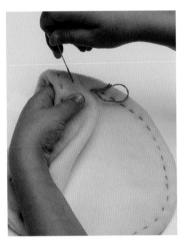 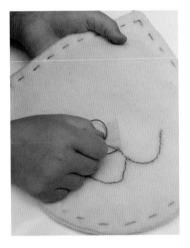

1. Using the templates on page 120 and following the instructions on page 116, cut out paper patterns for the bag, nose, and ears. Fold the fleece fabric in half and pin the bag pattern to it. Cut out. Remove the pins and pattern. You will have two bag shapes. Pin these together, right sides facing. Cut a length of embroidery floss (thread) and tie a knot at one end. Thread the needle. Sew backstitch (see page 116) all the way around the curved edge, leaving the top open. Finish with a knot, and trim the floss. Remove the pins.

2. Turn the bag the right way out. Fold over the top edge of the bag to the inside by about ½ in. (1 cm) and pin in place. Starting with a knot in colored embroidery floss and working from the inside of the bag, sew running stitch (see page 116) all the way around the top of the bag. Remove the pins as you sew. Finish with a knot inside the bag. Trim the floss.

3. Take another piece of embroidery floss and tie a knot at one end. Starting from the inside of the bag, sew running stitch around the curve of the bag. Finish with a knot inside the bag. Trim the floss.

4. Pin the paper pattern for the nose onto felt. Cut out. Remove the pins and pattern. Cut a length of floss in the second color, and tie a knot at one end. Thread the needle. Starting and finishing with a knot inside the bag, sew the felt nose onto the center of the bag using running stitch, ensuring you only sew through the front layer of the bag. Trim the floss. Embroider a mouth shape in backstitch in the same color, starting and finishing with a knot inside the bag. Finish with a knot on the inside. Trim floss.

5. Pin the pattern for the ear onto a fabric scrap. Cut out two. Remove pins and pattern. Pin the ears to the bag. Starting and finishing with a knot inside the bag, attach the ears with running stitch. Remove pins. Sew buttons on for the eyes (see page 118). For the handle, cut a 39 in. (100 cm) length of ribbon. Sew each end onto either side of the bag with a few stitches. Make a ribbon bow and sew it onto the bag, making a few stitches in the bag and then sew through the back of the ribbon a few times. Finish with a few small stitches.

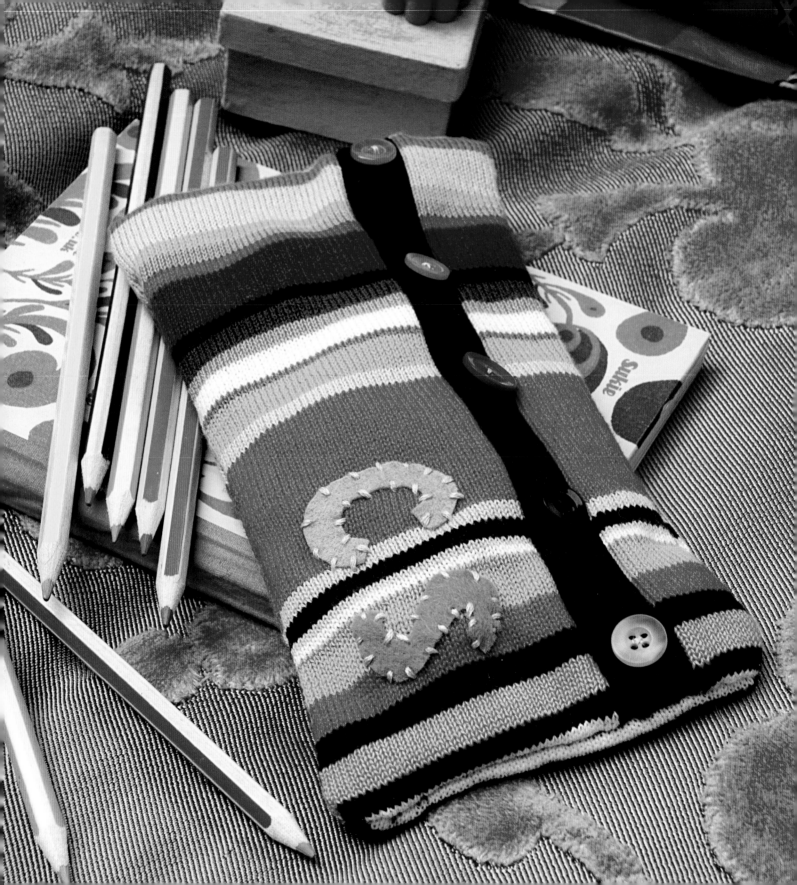

Cardigan Pencil Case

Recycle an old cardigan into a pencil case, making use of the buttons and buttonholes to form the opening. Make sure you check with an adult before cutting clothes, and keep all the scraps and off-cuts to use in other projects!

Materials

Pencil
Ruler
Paper
Scissors
Old cardigan with button fastenings (check with the owner if it is not yours!)
Pins
Embroidery floss (thread) and needle
Scraps of felt
Pen
Extra buttons, if needed

1. Using a pencil and ruler, draw a 6 x 10 in. (15 x 26 cm) rectangle onto paper. Cut out to make a paper pattern. Do the cardigan buttons up, turn it inside out, and lay it flat on the table. Pin the pattern through both layers of the cardigan, with the row of buttons about 2 in. (5 cm) from one long edge of the pattern.

2. Cut around the pattern with scissors. Remove the pins and pattern. Pin again to hold the two layers together.

3. Cut a length of embroidery floss (thread) and tie a knot at one end. Thread the needle. Sew around the rectangle using backstitch (see page 116). Finish with a knot and trim the floss.

4. Undo the buttons and turn your pencil case the right way out, pushing out the corners to make a nice rectangle. To add your initials to the case, draw letters onto the scraps of felt with a pen and cut out. Pin the letters to the front of the pencil case. Starting and finishing with a knot on the inside, slipstitch (see page 117) the letters in place with embroidery floss. Make sure you sew through only one layer of the pencil case. Trim the floss and remove the pins. Sew on extra buttons (see page 118) if there are any missing.

Felt Book Cover

These cute book covers make the perfect gift for grandparents, aunts, and uncles. Draw a picture onto fabric and then embroider it with backstitch. Sew it onto felt to make a cover for a notebook or favorite story to make a truly personalized gift that will be treasured for years to come.

Materials

Scissors
Plain cotton fabric
Embroidery hoop
Pencil
Embroidery floss (thread) in
    several colors and needle
Ruler
Pen
Felt
Pins
Rickrack and needle and thread
    (optional)
Buttons (optional)

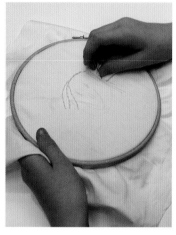

1. Cut out a square of cotton fabric, each side measuring about 3 in. (8 cm) more than the diameter of the embroidery hoop. Put it into the hoop, tightening the hoop so that the fabric is nice and taut (see page 118). Draw a picture on the fabric with a pencil.

2. Cut a length of embroidery floss (thread) and tie a knot at one end. Thread the needle. With the knot on the underside of the fabric, sew backstitch (see page 116) over the lines of your drawing, changing colors for different parts of the picture. Finish with a knot on the underside. Remove the embroidery from the hoop. Draw a square or rectangle around your picture using a pencil and ruler. Cut out.

3. Measure from the top to the bottom of your book and add ¾ in. (2 cm) to this measurement. Measure horizontally across the book, over the spine, and across the back, and add 3 in. (8 cm) to this measurement. With a pen and ruler, draw a rectangle with these measurements on the felt. Cut out. Fold over the short ends of the felt by 1½ in. (4 cm) and pin in place. This will give you the book flaps. Check that the cover will fit your book and alter the width of the flaps if you need to.

4. Starting and finishing with a knot on the inside, sew running stitch or blanket stitch (see page 116) around the edge of the felt. Remove the pins.

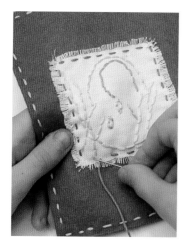

5. Pin your embroidery to the front of the felt cover. Use floss to sew it in place with running stich or cross stitch (see page 117), starting and finishing with a knot on the inside of the cover. Make sure you stitch through the front cover only and not through the inside flaps. Remove pins.

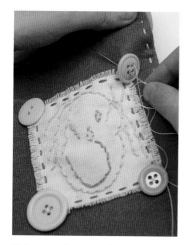

6. Sew on buttons (see page 118) for extra decoration if you like. Alternatively, sew rickrack around your embroidery with a needle and thread, starting and finishing with a few small stitches.

Pincushions

A must for every sewing kit, the ladybug and leaf pincushions are practical as well as cute. Make one or the other or stitch both of them and use one for pins and one for needles. Why not give them as presents to family and friends or stitch several to sell at a school fundraiser?

Materials

Paper and pencil, to make the pattern pieces
Scissors
Red and black felt for the ladybug
Pins
Green felt for the leaf
Embroidery floss (thread) – for the leaf, use floss in a slightly different color from the leaf
Needle
Fiberfill (stuffing)
2 buttons for the ladybug's eyes

1. Using the templates on page 123 and following the instructions on page 116, cut out one paper pattern for the ladybug's body, one for its head, and one for the leaf. Fold the red felt in half and pin the pattern for the ladybug's body to it. Cut out so that you have two identical red felt pieces. Pin the pattern for the ladybug's head to the black felt and cut out. Fold the green felt in half and pin the leaf pattern to it. Cut out so that you have two identical green felt pieces. Remove all pins and patterns.

2. Cut a length of embroidery floss (thread) and tie a knot at one end. Thread the needle. Starting on the underside of the felt and using running stitch (see page 116), sew the ladybug's head onto one of the body pieces. Finish with a knot on the underside of the felt. Trim the floss. Cut out small circles of black felt and sew them onto the ladybug's body in the same way.

3. Starting and finishing with a knot on the underside of the felt, sew a line of backstitch (see page 116) down the middle of the ladybug's body. Trim the floss. Make leaf vein markings on one of the leaf pieces in the same way with backstitch, using floss in a slightly different color from the felt.

4. Pin the front and back pieces of the ladybug together and stitch around them with running stitch, leaving a small opening. Remove the pins. Do the same with the leaf.

5. Push fiberfill (stuffing) through the opening to stuff the ladybug and leaf (see page 115). Use plenty of fiberfill so that the pincushion will be nice and plump. Sew the opening up and finish with a knot on the underside.

6. Following the instructions on page 118, sew buttons onto the ladybug's head so that they look like eyes.

Sewing Basket

Store your sewing things in style with a pretty sewing basket made from an old biscuit tin. It is made from circles of fabric that are gathered around the tin and creates the ideal place to keep scissors, thread, and other sewing essentials.

Materials

Old round metal container,
  about 7 in. (18 cm) in diameter
Cardboard
Pencil
Scissors
Fabric in 2 colors
Tape measure
Needle and thread
Craft glue
Batting (wadding)
Rickrack and braid
Ribbon for the handle

1. Place the metal container on the cardboard and draw around it with the pencil. Cut out the cardboard just inside the pencil line so that the cardboard circle will be slightly smaller than the container. Check that this fits inside the container, if it doesn't, trim it a little more. Put the cardboard to one side.

2. Place the container on the fabric. Measure the container depth and double it. Add 1½ in. (4 cm) to this measurement. Measure this total from the outside of the container and mark it on the fabric with a pencil. Keeping the same distance from the container, draw a circle all around the container. Move the container and cut around the circle. Cut a length of thread, and thread the needle. Sew a few small stitches in the fabric near the edge and sew large running stitches (see page 116) all the way around it.

3. Place the container in the middle of the fabric. Pull the thread and gather up the fabric around it. Finish with a few small stitches. Trim the thread.

4. To make the inside base of the container, place the cardboard circle onto a second piece of fabric. Measure 1½ in. (4 cm) out from the circle, then cut all around. Start with a few small stitches near the edge of the fabric circle, then sew running stitch around it, as in Step 2. Gather the fabric over the cardboard circle and finish with a few stitches in the fabric. Trim the thread.

5. Dab craft glue inside the base of the container and on the underside of the cardboard disc from Step 4. Push this disc inside the container. Arrange the folds of the fabric so that they are even and put something heavy inside the container until the glue dries (a bag of dried beans or rice will work well).

6. To make the inner lid, cut out a circle of cardboard using the metal lid as your guide, and cutting it slightly smaller, as you did in Step 1. Draw around this onto batting (wadding). Cut out the batting, and glue it to the cardboard. Cut out another piece of fabric that is 1½ in. (4 cm) bigger all around than the lid. Gather it up as you did before in Step 4 on the back of the padded disc. Sew a few small stitches to hold it in place and trim the thread.

7. Lay the metal lid onto a piece of fabric and again cut out a circle about 1½ in. (4 cm) bigger all around. Move the lid. Sew running stitch around the circle of fabric as before. Place the metal lid in the middle of the fabric. Pull the thread and gather up the fabric around it so that it sits neatly across the lid. Finish with a few small stitches and trim the thread.

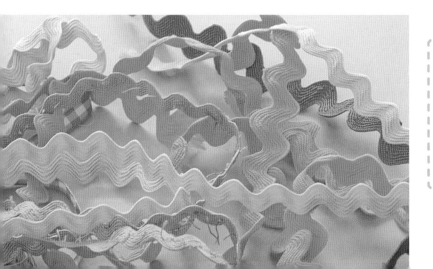

Tip

For this project three different fabrics were used, each with in a different color and pattern. Don't worry if you only have one type of fabric, the finished sewing basket will still look great. You can then glue on circles, squares, stars, or other shapes made from scraps of fabric to make it a bit more colorful, if you wish.

8. Spread glue inside the metal lid and on the underside of the padded disc and stick the disc in place. Again, it is a good idea to put something heavy on it until the glue dries.

9. Glue braid and rickrack around the top of the container and around the rim of the lid, overlapping the ends a little. To make the handle, tie a bow in the ribbon and glue it onto the top of the lid. Leave to dry.

Needle Case

Keep needles safe in this lovely needle case made from felt and decorated with a cherry motif using ribbon and buttons. Very easy to make, it is the perfect accompaniment to your sewing kit and also makes a charming gift for any avid sewer.

Materials

Paper and pencil, to make the pattern pieces
Ruler
Scissors
Pins
Felt in 3 colors
Pinking shears
Thin green ribbon
Needle and thread
Embroidery floss (thread) and needle
2 red buttons

1. Using the pencil and ruler, draw a rectangle measuring 6½ x 4¼ in. (17 x 11 cm) onto paper. Cut out the paper pattern and pin it to one of the felt pieces. Cut out the felt using pinking shears. This will be the cover of the needle case. Remove the pins and pattern.

2. Draw a rectangle measuring 3½ x 2¾ in. (9 x 7 cm) onto paper and cut out the pattern. Pin it to another color of felt. Cut it out using pinking shears so that it has a jagged edge. This will be the background for the cherry decoration on the front of the case. Remove the pins and the pattern.

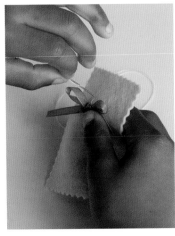

3. Take the ribbon and tie a bow in it. Trim the ends so that they are about 1¼ in. (3.5 cm) long. Cut a length of thread and knot it at one end. Thread the needle. Starting with the knot on the underside, use a few small stitches to secure the ribbon to the smaller felt rectangle. Finish with another knot on the back of the felt. Trim the thread.

4. Following the instructions on page 118, sew a red button with the needle and thread onto one end of the ribbon so that it looks like a cherry. Repeat on the other end.

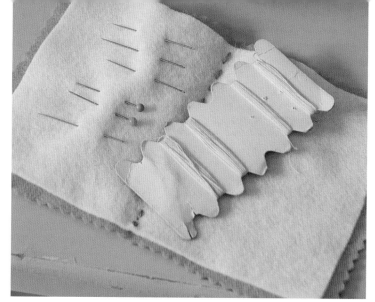

5. Take the larger felt rectangle (the cover) from Step 1 and fold it in half. Cut a length of embroidery floss (thread) and tie a knot at one end. Thread the needle. Starting with the knot at the back of the felt cover, sew the felt piece with cherries onto the front of it using running stitch (see page 116). Make sure that you sew through only one layer of the cover. Finish with a knot on the back. Trim the floss.

6. Using a pencil and ruler, draw another rectangle measuring 6 x 3¾ in. (15 x 9.5 cm) onto paper. Cut out the paper pattern and pin it to the third piece of felt. Cut out the felt with scissors. This will be the insert in the needle case. Remove the pins and pattern. Pin the insert down the middle of the inside of the cover piece. Knot the thread at one end. Starting from the underneath of the insert, sew running stitch to hold it in place. Finish with a knot on the back of the insert. Trim the floss. Remove the pins.

Barrette Holder

Need somewhere to store all your hair accessories? This cute barrette holder is the perfect thing! A pretty felt plant pot holds felt flowers decorated with French knots with ribbons to fasten on your hair slides. Buttons stitched onto the ribbon ends are the perfect spot to hang your bands on to keep them neat and tidy. For a variation try sewing on buttons or circles of felt instead of flowers.

Materials

Paper and pencil, to make the pattern pieces
Scissors
Brown felt
Pins
Embroidery floss (thread) and needle
Fiberfill (stuffing)
3 lengths of ribbon, each about 8 in. (20 cm) long, for attaching your barrettes (hair slides)
Colored felt for the flowers and leaves
Needle and thread
Thin ribbon for the loop
3 buttons

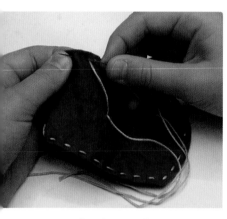

1. Using the templates on page 120 and following the instructions on page 116, cut out paper patterns for a flower, pot, and leaf. Fold the brown felt in half, pin the flowerpot pattern onto it and cut out. Remove the pins and pattern. You now have two flowerpot shapes. Pin them together. Cut a length of embroidery floss (thread) and tie a knot at one end. Thread the needle. Starting at one of the bottom corners and working from the back, sew running stitch (see page 116) around the sides and top of the pot. Finish with a knot on the back. Remove the pins and trim the floss.

2. Stuff the pot with fiberfill (stuffing), pushing it into the corner (see page 115).

3. Pin the ribbons inside the bottom of the pot. Starting and finishing with a knot on the back of the pot, sew running stitch across the bottom with embroidery floss. Trim the floss. Remove the pins as you work.

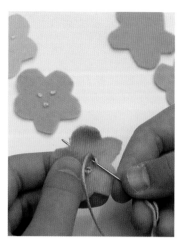

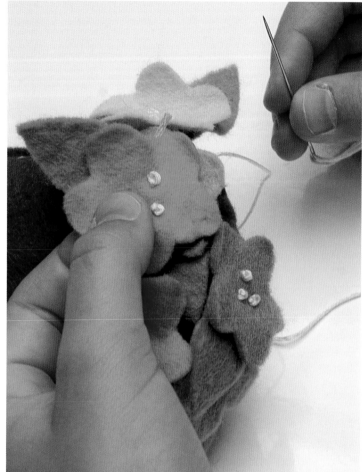

4. Pin the flower and leaf patterns from Step 1 onto colored felt. Cut out. Remove the pins and patterns. Repeat until you have about seven flowers and six leaves.

5. Starting and finishing with a knot on the back of the felt, sew French knots (see page 118) in the center of the flowers with floss. Trim the floss.

6. Cut a length of thread, and thread the needle. Sew a few small stitches on the top of the pot to hold the thread in place, then sew a leaf in position by stitching through the base of the leaf and back through the pot. Finish with a few small stitches. Trim the thread. Sew a flower onto the pot in the same way, stitching through the center of the flower. Try to keep the stitches small so that they will not show that much on the front of the flower. Sew the rest of the leaves and flowers onto the pot in the same way, overlapping them to make an attractive arrangement.

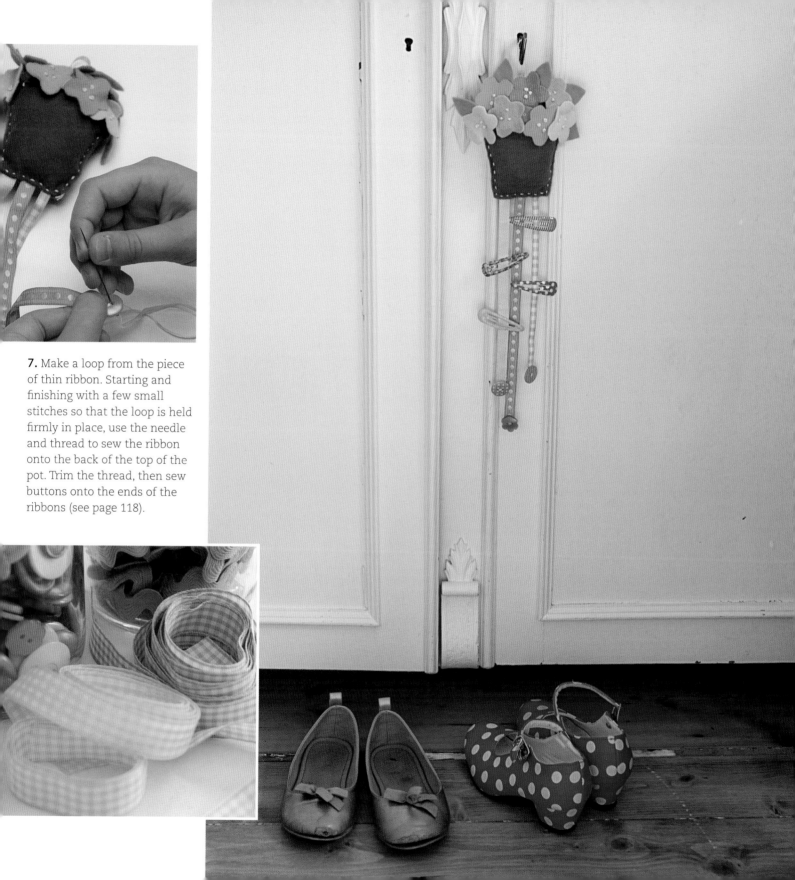

7. Make a loop from the piece of thin ribbon. Starting and finishing with a few small stitches so that the loop is held firmly in place, use the needle and thread to sew the ribbon onto the back of the top of the pot. Trim the thread, then sew buttons onto the ends of the ribbons (see page 118).

Appliqué Cushion

Decorate your room with a pretty appliquéd cushion that you made yourself. Cut out flowers and leaves and sew onto plain fabric or make your own designs using hand-drawn shapes. You could even personalize a cushion by cutting out your initials from patterned fabrics and stitching them in place. Add a handful of dried lavender when you fill the cushion to give it a beautiful scent.

Materials

Paper and pencil, to make the
    pattern pieces
Scissors
Pins
Scraps of patterned fabrics
Plain fabric for the cushion cover
Ruler
Embroidery floss (thread) and
    needle
3 buttons
Needle and thread
Fiberfill (stuffing)

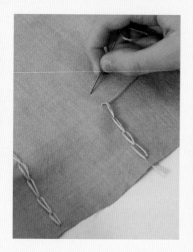

1. Using the templates on page 119 and following the instructions on page 116, cut out paper patterns for the flower and the circle. We cut out three flowers and three circles. Pin the patterns to scraps of fabric and cut out. Remove the pins and patterns. Set to one side.

2. Using the pencil and ruler, draw two rectangles measuring 14 x 10½ in. (35 x 27 cm) on the plain fabric. Cut out. Cut a length of embroidery floss (thread) and tie a knot at one end. Starting from the wrong side of the fabric, sew chain stitch (see page 117) onto the front of one of the rectangles to make three stalks from the bottom edge of the fabric up. Make the stalks between 3 in. (8 cm) and 4¾ in. (12 cm) long. Finish with knots on the wrong side and trim the thread. This is the front of the cushion cover.

3. Pin the fabric flowers and circles in place on the front of the cushion cover. Cut a length of thread, and thread the needle. Starting and finishing with a few small stitches, sew around the edges of the flowers and circles with running stitch (see page 116). Remove the pins.

4. For decoration, sew buttons onto the middle of the flowers (see page 118).

5. Pin the two fabric rectangles together, right sides facing, matching up the edges. Starting with a few small stitches, sew them together using backstitch (see page 116) all the way around, leaving a small opening of about 3 in. (8 cm). Remove the pins and the needle.

6. Turn the cushion cover the right way out, pulling the end of the thread to the outside. Stuff the cover with fiberfill (stuffing), pushing it into the corners (see page 115). Rethread the needle and slipstitch the opening closed.

Chapter 5

Dressing Up Time

Pirate Hat & Patch

Shiver me timbers! Have fun playing pirates with a great hat and eye patch that are so easy to make, leaving you plenty of time to play. Cut a square of spotty fabric and fold in half to make a necktie to complete your look.

Materials

Paper and pencil, to make the
   pattern pieces
Scissors
Pins
Black felt
White embroidery floss (thread)
   and needle
White felt
2 black buttons
Black thread and needle
Black elastic

1. Using the templates on page 124 and following the instructions on page 116, cut out a paper pattern for the front and the back of the hat. Pin these to the black felt and cut out one of each. Remove the pins and patterns.

2. Pin the two felt pieces together. Cut a length of white embroidery floss (thread) and tie a knot at one end. Thread the needle. Starting from the inside of the hat, use running stitch (see page 116) around the sides and top, leaving the bottom open. Finish with a knot on the inside, and trim the floss. Remove the pins.

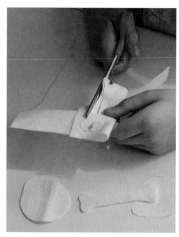

3. Using the templates on page 124, cut out paper patterns for one skull and two bones. Pin these to the white felt and cut out. Remove pins and patterns.

4. Pin the felt skull to the front of the hat near the top and in the middle, and one of the bones diagonally beneath it. Sew them in place with white floss using running stitch, starting and finishing with knots on the inside of the hat. Remove the pins. Pin the second bone diagonally over the top of the first to make a cross and sew onto the hat in the same way. Remove the pins.

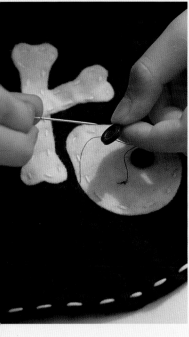

5. Sew on two buttons for the eye sockets with black thread (see page 118 for instructions).

6. Using the template on page 124, cut out a paper pattern for the eye patch. Fold the black felt and pin the pattern to it. Cut out. You will have two eye-patch shapes. Remove the pins and pattern. Cut a length of black thread and tie a knot at one end. Using small stitches, sew one end of the elastic to the top corner of one of the felt pieces, finishing with a knot on the same side as the first knot. Check the elastic will fit around your head, then sew the other end to the opposite top corner of the felt. Make sure the elastic is stitched securely in place.

7. Pin the second felt piece to the back of the first, hiding the elastic knots. Cut a length of white embroidery floss and tie a knot at one end. Thread the needle. Working from the back, use running stitch around the edges to join the felt pieces together. Finish with a knot on the back of the patch and trim the floss. Remove the pins.

Horse & Sheriff's Badge

Howdy partner! Choose a big sock, stuff it, and tie it onto a broomstick to make a horse to ride. Sew strips of fabric for the mane and add buttons for eyes. For the badge sew on an 'S' for sheriff or your own initial to complete the look.

Materials

FOR THE HORSE
Old sock, preferably an adult's (make sure you ask permission to use it first)
Fiberfill (stuffing)
Scissors
Fabric
Yarn (wool) and needle with a large eye
Paper and pencil, to make the pattern pieces
Pins
Felt for the ears
2 buttons
Craft glue
Broom handle

EXTARS FOR THE BADGE
Felt
Embroidery floss (thread) and needle
Needle and thread
Safety pin
5 small buttons

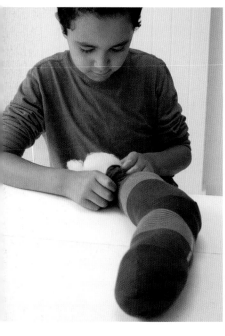

1. Take the sock and stuff it with fiberfill (stuffing) to form the horse's head (see page 115). Try to make sure that there are no lumps and bumps.

2. To make your horse's mane, tear strips of fabric about 1 in. (2–3 cm) wide, then cut them into lengths about 6 in. (15 cm) long. We used five different pieces of fabric, each with a different design, but feel free to use as many or as few as you wish.

3. Thread a length of yarn (wool) through the large needle. Starting and finishing with a knot in the yarn, make stitches through the middle of the strips all the way down the back of the sock. Finish with a knot and trim the yarn.

4. Follow the instructions on page 116 and use the template on page 123 to cut out the paper pattern for the ear. Fold the felt in half and pin the pattern onto it. Cut out to give you two ears. Remove the pins and pattern. Starting and finishing with a knot in the yarn, sew them in position on the horse's head with running stitch (see page 116).

5. Cut a length of yarn and tie a knot at one end. Thread the large needle. Following the instructions on page 118, sew on two buttons for the eyes.

6. Apply craft glue to the broom handle. Push the handle carefully inside the horse's head and press the sock down onto it to hold the sock in place.

Tie a double thickness of yarn around the base of the sock with a double knot and then a bow so that the head will be even more secure.

Tip

To stop the end of the broom handle scratching the floor take the second sock from the pair (or find an odd sock that you can use) and cut the toe off. Put a small clump of fiberfill in it. Put it over the bottom end of the handle, tying it in place with a length of wool.

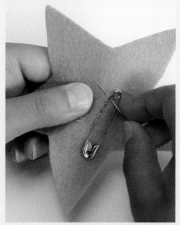

7. To make your sheriff's badge, use the template for the star shape on page 124 and cut out a paper pattern. Fold the felt in half and pin the pattern to it. Cut out. Remove the pins and pattern. You now have two star shapes. Cut a length of embroidery floss (thread) and tie a knot at one end. Thread the needle. Starting from the back of one of the stars, sew a letter with backstitch (see page 116)—either an "S" for "Sheriff" or the first letter of your name. Finish with a knot on the back of the star. Trim the floss.

8. Cut a length of thread, and thread the needle. Sew a few small stitches in the middle of the other star shape to hold the thread in place. Position the closed safety pin. Stitch over the part of the safety pin that doesn't move so that the safety pin and star are firmly held together. Finish with a few small stitches and trim thread.

9. Pin the two stars together, matching up the points of the stars. Starting and finishing with a few small stitches, use the needle and thread to slipstitch (see page 117) all the way around the star.

10. Sew a button on the end of each point of the star (see page 118). Giddyup, horse, and off you go!

Cell Phone

Put your button collection to good use with this great phone, which is perfect for making all those important calls. Embroider numbers onto the screen using backstitch or sew your name or initials on. If you want to give this as a gift to a baby, sew circles of felt instead of buttons, using different colors for a bright and cheery look.

Materials

Paper and pencil, to make the pattern pieces
Scissors
Pins
Felt in 4 colors
Embroidery floss (thread) and needle
Fiberfill (stuffing)
10 buttons

1. Using the templates on page 121 and following the instructions on page 116, cut out two paper patterns for the body of the phone, and one each for the screen, keypad, and front. Pin the patterns to the felt and cut out. Remove the pins and patterns.

2. To make the phone screen, cut a length of embroidery floss (thread) and tie a knot at one end. Thread the needle. Starting on the underside of the felt, use backstitch (see page 116) to sew numbers, such as 1, 2, 3, or letters, perhaps to spell your name. Finish with a knot on the back of the felt. Trim the floss.

3. Pin the screen and the keypad onto the phone front. Starting with a knot on the back, use running stitch (see page 116) to sew them in place. Finish with a knot on the back and trim the floss. Remove pins.

4. Pin the panel from Step 3 onto one of the phone body pieces and sew it in place with running stitch as before. Remove the pins. Pin the other phone body piece to the back of the first one and sew them together with running stitch. Leave a small opening in the side for the fiberfill (stuffing). Remove the pins.

5. Stuff the phone by pushing fiberfill through the hole, making sure that you push it well into all the corners (see page 115).

6. Sew up the opening. Sew buttons onto the keypad following the instructions on page 118.

Animal Hat

These furry animal hats are so cozy you won't want to take them off. Fur material is available from fabric stores in a range of different animal prints and is fun to use as it doesn't fray and is easy to cut. Why not make a tail as well? Simply cut a strip of fur fabric and sew it onto a piece of ribbon long enough to tie around your waist.

Materials

Paper and pencil, to make the pattern pieces
Scissors
Pins
Fake fur
Scraps of felt
Needle and thread

1. Using the templates on page 119 and following the instructions on page 116, cut out a paper pattern for the front of the hat, one for the back, and one for the bear ear. Pin the pattern pieces to the fake fur (you may find it easier to pin them to the back of the fur) and cut out. You will need four ears. Remove the pins and the patterns and set the front and back pieces aside.

2. Using the template on page 119, cut out a paper pattern for the bear inner ear. Pin the pattern to the felt and cut out two inner ears. Pin a felt inner ear to two of the fur ears. Cut a length of thread and tie a knot at one end. Thread the needle. Working from the back of the fur ear, sew the inner ears to the two fur ears with running stitch (see page 116). Finish with a knot on the back and trim the thread. Remove the pins. Sew the two remaining fur ears onto the back of these ears in the same way with running stitch.

3. Lay the back part of the fur hat flat on the table with the furry side up. Position the ears on top of the fur so that the straight edges are touching the top edge of the back piece, and pin together. Knot one end of the thread again and, working from the back of the hat, sew the ears in place with a few running stitches. Finish with a knot on the back of the hat and trim the thread. Remove the pins.

4. Lay the front of the hat onto the back, furry sides together. Pin the layers together, leaving the flat edge open. Sew them together using running stitch, starting and ending with a few small stitches to hold the thread in place. Turn the hat the right way out and put it on your head! If you want to make a tiger hat too, use the tiger ear templates on page 119 instead of the bear ones.

Tiara & Wand

Be the prettiest princess at the ball with this lovely tiara and beautiful butterfly wand. Cut jewel shapes from felt or sew beads and sequins on the tiara for a glittery look. (Make crowns in the same way using gold-colored felt, cut-out felt shapes, and buttons.) Try the tiara on before sewing the ends together to get a snug fit.

Materials

FOR THE TIARA
Paper and pencil, to make the pattern pieces
Scissors
Felt
Pins
Scraps of felt for the jewel decoration
Embroidery floss (thread) and needle

For the tiara

1. Using the template on page 122 and following the instructions on page 116, cut out a paper pattern for the tiara. Fold the felt in half and pin the pattern onto it, placing the fold line on the fold of the felt (see page 116). Cut out two of these shapes with scissors. Remove the pins and pattern.

2. Cut out jewel shapes—you can either use the heart and circle templates on page 119 or draw your own. The tiara shown here has five jewels altogether but you could give yours as many as you like. Pin the jewels to one of the tiara pieces. Cut a length of embroidery floss (thread) and tie a knot at one end. Thread the needle. Working from the wrong side of the tiara, slipstitch (see page 117) the jewels in place. Finish with a knot on the wrong side of the tiara.

3. Pin the two tiara pieces together. Use embroidery floss to sew them together with running stitch (see page 116), starting and finishing with a knot on the wrong side.

4. Wrap the tiara around your head to check the size, overlapping the ends as much as you need to so that it will be comfortable but won't fall off. Remove the tiara from your head, holding the felt where you want the overlap to be. Sew the ends of the tiara together to the correct size using a few stitches of embroidery floss, starting and finishing with a knot on the inside.

Materials

EXTRAS FOR THE WAND
Felt in 2 colors
Sequins and beads
Needle and thread
Wooden chopstick or skewer
  (make sure it doesn't have
  pointy ends)
Craft glue
Ribbons

Variation

Instead of attaching your butterfly to the chopstick or skewer, why not make a pretty brooch? Follow the instructions in step 7 on page 99 and stitch a safety pin onto the back of the the butterfly. Clip the finished piece to your favorite coat, sweater, bag, or anything else that you think will look great with a fluttering friend attached to it.

For the wand

1. Using the templates on page 120, cut out a paper pattern for the butterfly wings and body. Fold one of the pieces of felt in half. Pin the wings pattern to it with the long edge of the pattern on the fold (see page 116). Cut around the shape. Repeat to give you a second pair of wings. Remove the pins and pattern.

2. Add decoration to your wand by sewing sequins and beads (see page 118) with the needle and thread onto one set of butterfly wings. Next, fold the felt in the second color in half and pin the paper pattern of the butterfly body to it. Cut out. This will give you two felt body shapes. Remove the pins and the pattern.

3. Pin the wing pieces together, and then pin a body piece to the front and back of the wings in the middle. Cut a length of embroidery floss (thread) and tie a knot at one end. Thread the needle. With the knot at the back of the butterfly, sew the wing and body pieces together with running stitch (see page 116), leaving a gap at the bottom of the body. Finish with a knot on the back of the butterfly. Trim the floss. Remove the pins.

4. Push the wooden chopstick or skewer into the body of the butterfly and stick in place with a dab of craft glue. Tie ribbons around the wand, securing them in place with glue.

Clown Hat & Ruff

Amuse your friends with a funny clown outfit that is simple to make. For even speedier results, sew three big buttons or circles of felt onto the hat instead of making pompoms. Fleece fabric is great to sew with as it doesn't fray and holds its shape quite well, which is important as you want your hat to stand up nice and straight.

Materials

Paper and pencil, to make the pattern pieces
Scissors
Sticky tape
Fleece fabric
Pins
Needle and thread
Rickrack
Pencil and compass
Ruler
Cardboard (an empty cereal packet is ideal)
Yarn (wool) for the pompoms in 3 different colors
Needle with a large eye (for the pompoms)
Fabric for the ruff
Pinking shears
Safety pin
Elastic about ⅛ in. (3 mm) wide

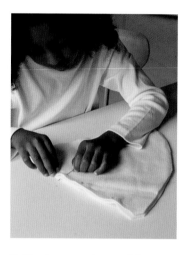

1. Using the template on page 126 and following the instructions on page 116, cut out two paper patterns for the clown hat and tape them together along the dotted line marked on the template to make one large pattern. Fold the fleece fabric in half and pin the hat pattern onto it. Cut out. Remove the pins and pattern. You will now have two fleece hat shapes.

2. Pin the two pieces of fleece together along both straight sides. Cut a length of thread, and thread the needle. Starting with a few small stitches to hold the thread in place, sew backstitch (see page 116) along both straight sides. Finish with a few small stitches then trim the thread.

3. Turn the hat the right way out. Pin a length of rickrack about ½ in. (1 cm) from the bottom edge of the hat, and overlap the ends a little. Starting and finishing with a few small stitches, sew it in place with running stitch (see page 116). Remove the pins. Trim the thread.

4. To make the pompoms, set the compass to 1¼ in. (3 cm) and draw two circles onto cardboard. They will both have a diameter of 2½ in. (6 cm). Reset the compass to ½ in. (1 cm) and draw a smaller circle in the middle of both of the big circles. Cut out around the circle lines to give you two donut shapes. Holding the shapes together, start to wrap the yarn (wool) around them (see page 118). Continue until the inner hole is full of yarn. Follow the instructions on page 118 to make three pompoms in total, each in a different color.

5. Take one end of the length of yarn tied around the middle of a pompom and thread it through the needle with the large eye. Use this to stitch the pompom onto the front of the hat, making sure that you sew through only one layer. Stitch back through the middle of the pompom and through the hat a few times to hold the pompom in place. Finish with a knot inside the hat and trim the yarn. Repeat for the other two pompoms. Your hat is now ready to wear!

6. For the ruff, take the fabric and, using the pencil and ruler, draw a rectangle measuring about 43 in. (110 cm) long and 6½ in. (16 cm) wide. Cut out with pinking shears so the fabric won't fray. Fold over one long side of the fabric by about 1 in. (2.5 cm) to the wrong side and pin. Starting and finishing with a few small stitches, sew running stitch with the needle and thread all the way along, close to the raw edge. This will form a channel along the fabric. Remove the pins. Trim the thread.

7. For extra decoration, pin the rickrack (you will need a piece as long as your ruff fabric) along the front of the fabric, about ½ in. (1 cm) in from the bottom edge. Starting and finishing with a few small stitches, sew the rickrack in place with running stitch. Trim the thread.

8. Cut a piece of elastic about 16 in. (40 cm) long and fasten a safety pin through one end. Push the pin through the channel in the fabric, gathering up the fabric as you go and keeping hold of the other end of elastic. Continue pushing until the pin comes out the other end of the channel.

9. Pull both ends of the elastic and remove the pin. Tie the ends together in a knot and then even out the gathers on the ruff.

Fairy Wings

Perfect for all budding butterflies and fairies, these pretty wings are very easy to make, although little hands may need some help to gather up the netting. Sew small bows all over the wings to decorate them, or leave them plain for even speedier results.

Materials

Pink net, measuring 59 in. (150 cm) long by the standard width
Pins
Scissors
Wide pink ribbon for the wings
Embroidery floss (thread) and needle
Narrow ribbon for the bows

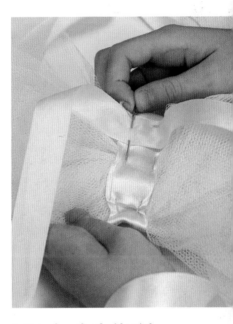

1. Lay out the net on the table (or floor) and gather it up into a long sausage shape. Fold the ends into the middle, overlapping them slightly. Pin to hold in place.

2. Cut a piece of the wide pink ribbon about 7 in. (18 cm) long. Wrap it around the middle of the net and, removing the pins from the net, pin the ribbon in place.

3. Cut a length of embroidery floss (thread) and tie a knot at one end. Thread the needle. Working from the underside, stitch through all the layers so that the ribbon is firmly held in place. Trim the floss and remove the pins.

4. Cut a length of wide pink ribbon 94 in. (240 cm) long. Find the middle of the ribbon. Starting and finishing with knots in the floss, sew the middle of the ribbon horizontally across the ribbon stitched around the net (see Step 3), with a few small stitches. Trim the floss.

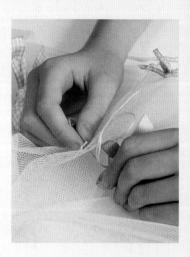

5. Cut the narrow ribbon into lengths about 12 in. (30 cm) long. Tie them into bows. Tie a knot at one end of the embroidery floss and, working from the underside, sew a bow onto the wings, stitching through the net and the ribbon a few times and finishing with a knot on the underside. Trim the floss. Sew the other ribbon bows onto the wings in the same way.

6. To wear the wings, ask someone to hold them against your back for you. Pull the ends of the wide pink ribbon over your shoulders and cross them over your chest. Wrap them around your back and then bring them around to your front. Tie them in a pretty bow.

Techniques

Your sewing kit

Before you start to sew, you will need to put together a sewing kit. A few basic tools, kept in a box or basket, will keep everything to hand ready for when you start your next project. Sewing baskets are available from haberdashery and craft stores, or why not make one yourself (see page 78)?

Scissors—It is a good idea to have two pairs of scissors, one for fabric and thread, which need to be kept nice and sharp, and one for cutting paper.

Tape measure—You will need a tape measure or ruler for taking measurements and checking sizes.

Pins—Pins are essential for holding fabric layers together while you stitch. Keep them in a pincushion when you are not using them. Safety pins are useful for threading ribbons and elastic.

Needles—Needles are available in a range of sizes to be used with different fabrics and threads. Try to buy a set with a variety of needles in it so you always have a suitable one to hand.

Needle threader—These are available from haberdashery stores, and whilst they are not essential, they are very handy.

Threads—Cotton thread is available in a wide range of colors. Have a few reels of cotton in your sewing basket in a selection of colors ready for use. Embroidery floss (thread) is used for decorative stitching and again is available in lots of colors.

Pencil or pen—Essential for marking the position of buttons or beads. Haberdashery stores sell air-soluble pens, which are very useful as the marks disappear after a few minutes.

Buttons—Start collecting spare buttons and keep them in a jar so you always have some to hand. Save buttons from clothes that are too worn to be passed on and check out yard sales and charity shops, where you often find boxes and bags of buttons.

Ribbons and braids—These are very handy for finishing off projects. Stash giftwrapping ribbons away to be used at a later date. Even short lengths of ribbon can come in handy, so keep any scraps that you can get your hands on.

Fabrics—There are a huge range of fabrics available from fabric stores in lots of great colors and patterns. Cotton fabrics, felt, and fleece are all easy to work with and are great to use for your sewing projects. Recycling your old clothes is also a good source of fabric; save odd socks and gloves too.

Patterned cotton fabrics have a right side and a wrong side. The right side is the patterned side and the wrong side is the back of the fabric (the side without pattern).

Fiberfill (stuffing)—This is available from haberdashery stores and is used for filling soft toys and making padded projects. When you are stuffing a sewing project, pull off small bits of fiberfill rather than using large handfuls and push them inside. Use the blunt end of a pencil or a knitting needle to push the fiberfill into corners and thin areas if you need to.

How to use a pattern

There are lots of templates in this book to help you make the projects. To use them you will need some tracing paper or thin paper that you can see through plus a pencil or pen. Trace around the template you want to use and cut it out. Either pin this pattern onto your fabric or draw around it onto thicker paper to make a pattern that is easier to use and more durable when cut out. Pin the pattern onto your fabric, making sure that the fabric is nice and flat with no creases. Position the pattern close to the edges of the fabric so that you don't waste any. If you need two pieces that are the same shape, fold the fabric over and pin the pattern onto it. Some of the patterns in this book have a dotted Fold line on them. To use these fold the fabric over and pin the pattern piece onto it, positioning the fold line on the pattern along the fold of the fabric. This will double the shape when it is cut out. Cut around the pattern as close to the edge as you can, then remove the pins and the pattern.

Threading a needle

Firstly, choose a needle that is right for the job. Look at the eye of the needle (the hole at the top) and check that it is big enough to fit the thread that you are using. Cut a piece of thread about 25 in. (65 cm) long. Flatten the end of the thread slightly between your fingers and then push it through the eye of the needle. If using thread, snip the end to make it nice and blunt and thread through the eye. To make it easier, lean your arms against the table to steady them. Pull about 6 in. (15 cm) of the thread through the needle. You are now ready to sew.

You can buy needle threaders from haberdashery stores, which make the job easier. Take the needle threader and push the wire part through the eye of the needle. Pull the end of your thread through the wire and pull the needle threader back through the needle eye: the thread will follow.

Starting and finishing stitching

It is important to start and end your sewing properly to stop it coming undone. If you are using embroidery floss (thread), take the floss and tie two knots on top of each other near the end. Trim the end to about ¼ in. (5 mm). Place the needle under the fabric and push it through to the front in the position where you want the first stitch. Continue sewing your chosen stitch. To finish, tie knot on the underside and trim the floss.

If you are sewing with thread, start by making a few small stitches on top of each other on the wrong side of the fabric. Push the needle through to the right side of the fabric to begin sewing.

Running stitch

This is the simplest stitch and can be used in embroidery and for joining two layers of fabric together. It is very easy to do but not very strong. Starting with a few small stitches or a knot to secure the end of the thread, push the needle down through the fabric a little way along and pull the thread as far as it will go. Then bring the needle back up through the fabric a little way along and repeat to form a row of stitches. Try to keep the stitches even and neat. Finish with a few small stitches or a knot.

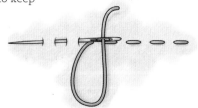

Backstitch

This is a very useful stitch as it is strong and similar to the stitches used on a sewing machine. It makes a solid line of stitches. Pull the needle through to the front of the fabric and insert the needle back through the fabric to the left of this. Pull the thread and bring the needle up through the fabric again a stitch width away on the right of this first stitch. Insert the needle back at the end of the first stitch and continue to create a neat line of stitches.

Chain stitch

This is a very pretty stitch that can be used in lines or made into Lazy Daisies. Bring the needle up through the fabric (having tied a knot in the end) and push the needle back through next to the thread.

Leave a small loop in the thread and bring the needle up through the loop and pull the thread through. Repeat this, working from right to left, to create a line of chain stitch. To make a Lazy Daisy, group 5 or 6 chain stitches together in a small circle. Finish with a knot on the underside of the fabric or a few small stitches.

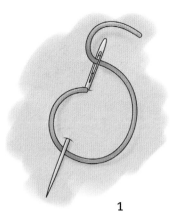 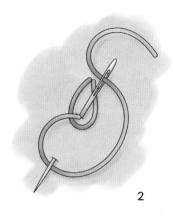

1   **2**

Blanket stitch

This stitch is used to create a decorative edging to fabric. Tie a knot at the end of the thread and bring the thread through at the edge of the fabric. Push the needle back through the fabric a short distance from the edge and loop the thread under the needle. Pull the needle and thread as far as you can to make the first stitch. Make another stitch to the right of this and again loop the thread under the needle. Continue along the fabric and finish with a few small stitches or a knot on the underside.

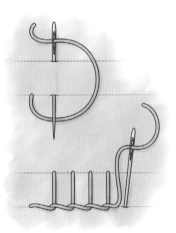

Slipstitch or whip stitch

This stitch is used to sew two layers together and close up gaps in seams. Start with a knot or a few small stitches and then bring the needle through both layers of fabric, from the back to the front, a few millimetres from the edge, and pull the thread through. Take the needle back to the underside of the fabric again and make another stitch a little way from the first. Continue making stitches and finish with a knot or a few small stitches and trim the thread.

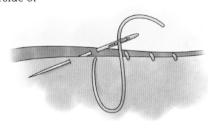

Cross stitch

Cross stitch is a lovely decorative stitch, which can be used on its own or in groups to make pictures and pretty borders for your projects.

1 Tie a knot in the floss and push the needle from the back to the front of the fabric. Next, insert the needle to make a diagonal stitch.

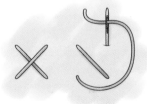

2 Bring the needle back through the fabric in line with the bottom of the first stitch and make another diagonal stitch crossing the first.

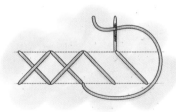

3 If making a line of crossstitch, sew a line of the first diagonal stitch working from left to right and then embroider the second stitch working from right to left across all of them. Always make the crosses in the same direction. Finish with a knot on the underside and trim the thread.

French knot

This stitch makes a raised dot and is a great decorative stitch. Tie a knot in the end of the embroidery floss (thread) and push the needle from the back to the front of the fabric. Hold the end of the needle in your right hand and wind the floss around it once (or twice for a bigger knot). Still holding the floss, push the needle back through the fabric as close as you can to where you began. Pull the thread through from the back to form the knot. Tie a knot in the underside of the fabric and cut the thread.

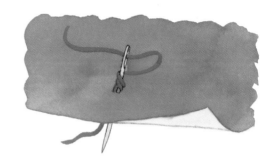

Making a pompom

Cut two cardboard circles to the size required and cut out small circles in the middle of them. Hold the discs together and wrap the yarn (wool) around them until the inner hole is full of yarn. With a pair of scissors, cut around the edge of the fluffy circle, pushing the blade of the scissors between the two cardboard discs. Cut all the way round and pull a double length of yarn between the cardboard discs. Tie a tight knot in it, leaving a long tail of yarn. Pull the cardboard discs off the pompom (you can snip the disc off with scissors if you need to). Fluff up the pompom and trim it slightly to make a nice round shape, keeping the long ties to use to sew the pompom in place.

Sewing on a button

Mark the place where you want the button to be and make a few small stitches to secure the thread on the wrong side of the fabric. Bring the needle through this point from the back of the fabric and through one of the holes in the button. Push the needle back through the second hole and down through the fabric. Repeat this five or six times. The needle holes should be close together, so angle the needle toward the center of the button from each hole. Finish on the back of the fabric, and sew a few small stitches over each other and trim the thread.

Sewing on beads and sequins

Beads and sequins can add the final decorative touch to your sewing projects. Start with a few small stitches underneath where the first bead will go. Thread the needle through the bead or sequin and push the bead or sequin flat onto the fabric. Insert the needle back into the fabric slightly underneath the bead or sequin and pull through. Continue in the same way, and to finish make a few small stitches on the back of the fabric, then trim the thread. To make the sequins more secure, sew two stitches through them on opposite sides and finish in the same way.

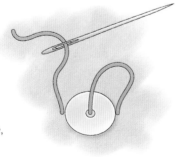

Using an embroidery hoop

Embroidery hoops are used to hold your fabric taut while you embroider. The fabric is placed between two hoops, which can be tightened to keep floppy and lightweight fabrics nice and smooth, making them much easier to work on.

Templates

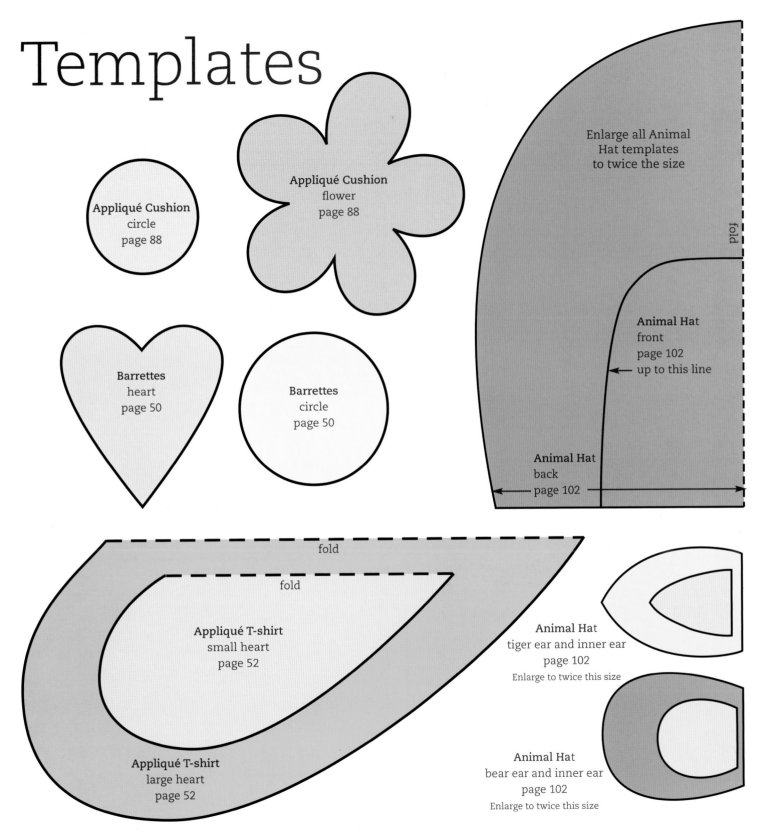

Appliqué Cushion
circle
page 88

Appliqué Cushion
flower
page 88

Enlarge all Animal
Hat templates
to twice the size

fold

Animal Hat
front
page 102
← up to this line

Animal Hat
back
page 102

Barrettes
heart
page 50

Barrettes
circle
page 50

fold

fold

Appliqué T-shirt
small heart
page 52

Appliqué T-shirt
large heart
page 52

Animal Hat
tiger ear and inner ear
page 102
Enlarge to twice this size

Animal Hat
bear ear and inner ear
page 102
Enlarge to twice this size

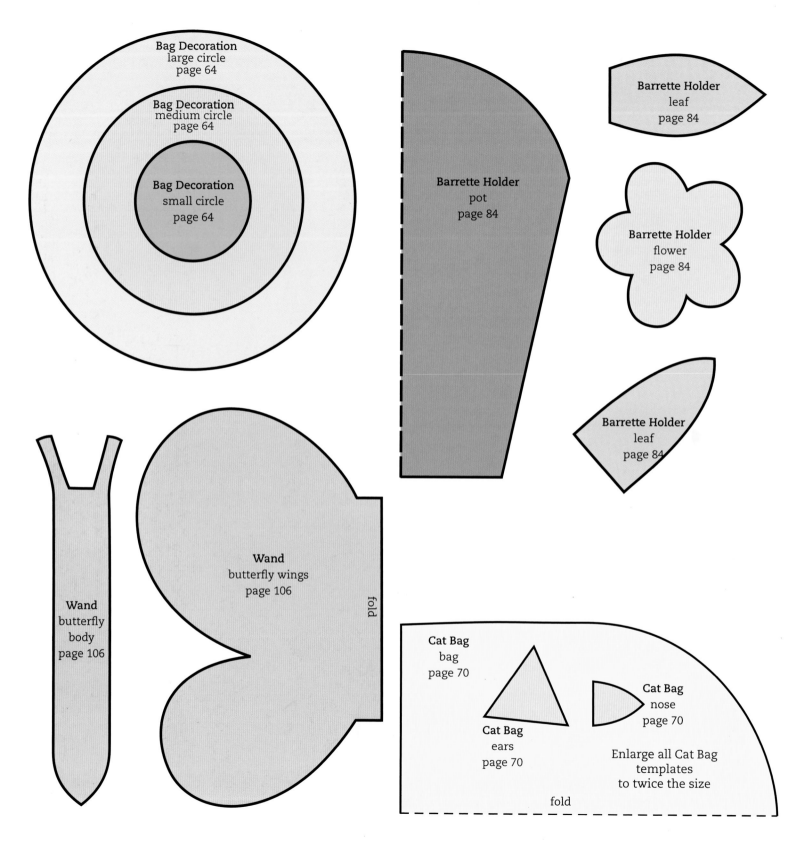

Bag Decoration
large circle
page 64

Bag Decoration
medium circle
page 64

Bag Decoration
small circle
page 64

Barrette Holder
leaf
page 84

Barrette Holder
pot
page 84

Barrette Holder
flower
page 84

Barrette Holder
leaf
page 84

Wand
butterfly wings
page 106

fold

Wand
butterfly
body
page 106

Cat Bag
bag
page 70

Cat Bag
nose
page 70

Cat Bag
ears
page 70

Enlarge all Cat Bag
templates
to twice the size

fold

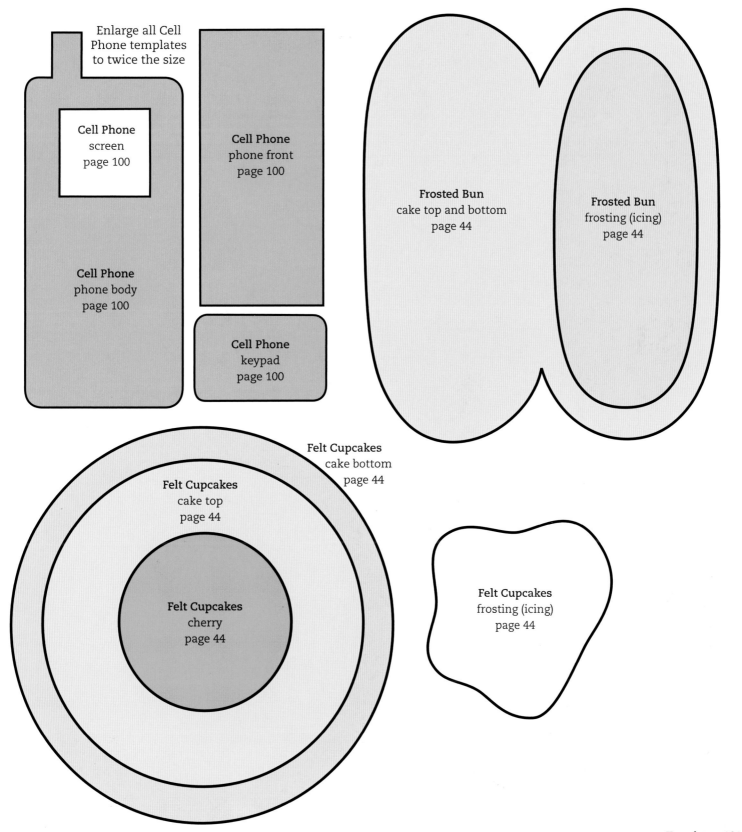

Enlarge all Cell
Phone templates
to twice the size

Cell Phone
screen
page 100

Cell Phone
phone front
page 100

Cell Phone
phone body
page 100

Cell Phone
keypad
page 100

Frosted Bun
cake top and bottom
page 44

Frosted Bun
frosting (icing)
page 44

Felt Cupcakes
cake bottom
page 44

Felt Cupcakes
cake top
page 44

Felt Cupcakes
cherry
page 44

Felt Cupcakes
frosting (icing)
page 44

Finger Puppet Animal Features

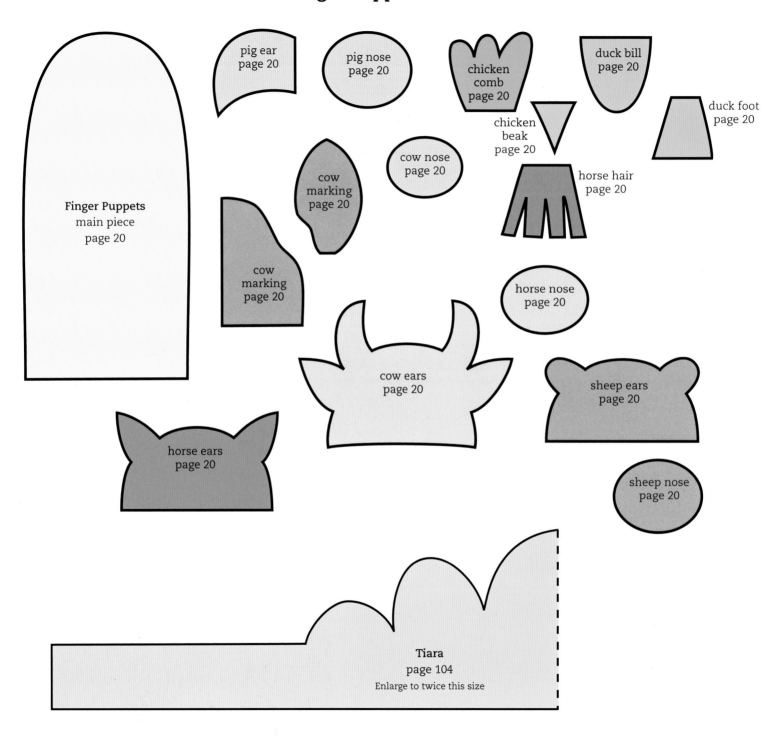

pig ear
page 20

pig nose
page 20

chicken
comb
page 20

duck bill
page 20

chicken
beak
page 20

duck foot
page 20

cow nose
page 20

cow
marking
page 20

horse hair
page 20

Finger Puppets
main piece
page 20

cow
marking
page 20

horse nose
page 20

cow ears
page 20

sheep ears
page 20

horse ears
page 20

sheep nose
page 20

Tiara
page 104
Enlarge to twice this size

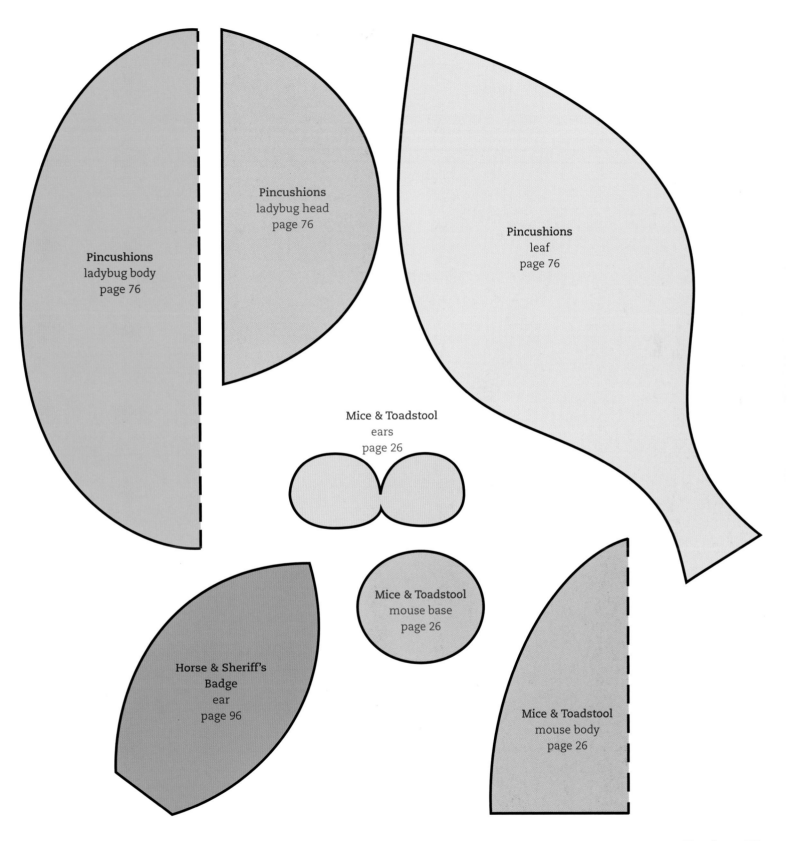

Pincushions
ladybug body
page 76

Pincushions
ladybug head
page 76

Pincushions
leaf
page 76

Mice & Toadstool
ears
page 26

Mice & Toadstool
mouse base
page 26

**Horse & Sheriff's
Badge**
ear
page 96

Mice & Toadstool
mouse body
page 26

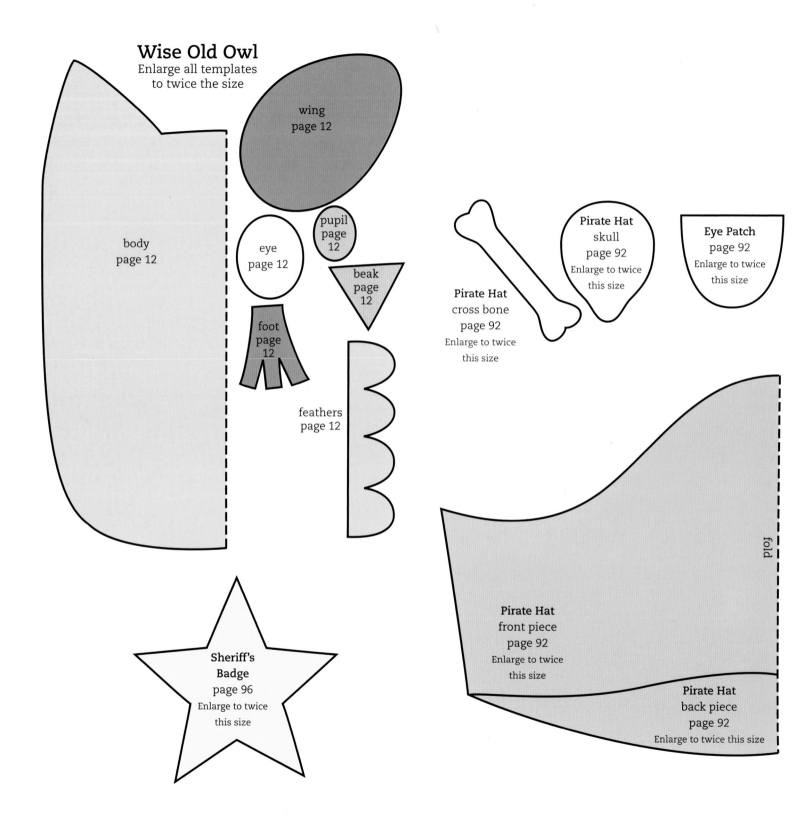

Wise Old Owl

Enlarge all templates to twice the size

wing
page 12

body
page 12

pupil
page 12

eye
page 12

beak
page 12

foot
page 12

feathers
page 12

Pirate Hat
cross bone
page 92
Enlarge to twice
this size

Pirate Hat
skull
page 92
Enlarge to twice
this size

Eye Patch
page 92
Enlarge to twice
this size

Sheriff's
Badge
page 96
Enlarge to twice
this size

Pirate Hat
front piece
page 92
Enlarge to twice
this size

Pirate Hat
back piece
page 92
Enlarge to twice this size

fold

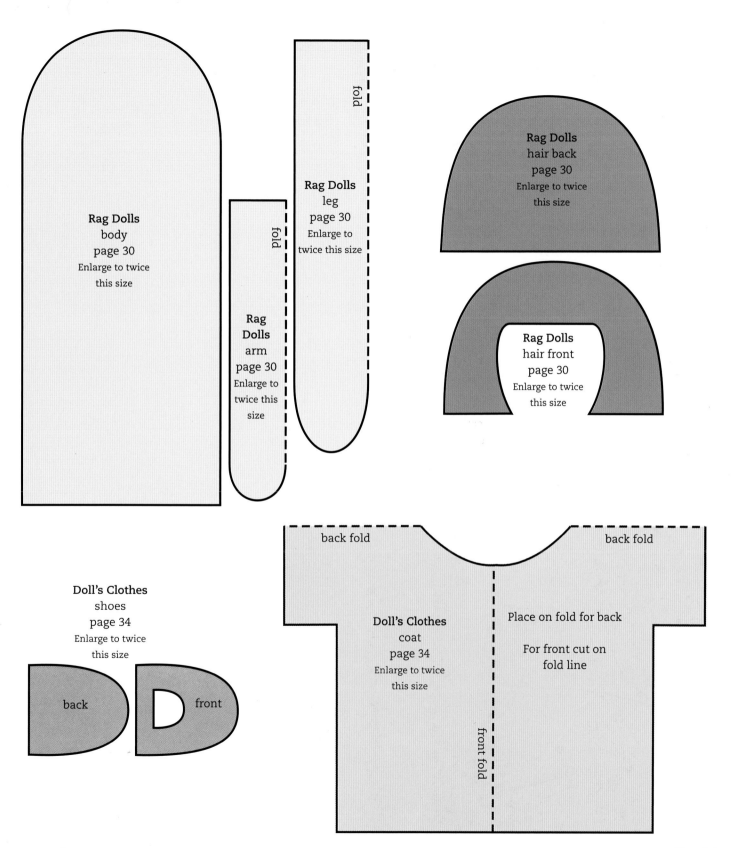

Rag Dolls
body
page 30
Enlarge to twice
this size

fold

Rag Dolls
leg
page 30
Enlarge to
twice this size

fold

Rag Dolls
arm
page 30
Enlarge to
twice this
size

Rag Dolls
hair back
page 30
Enlarge to twice
this size

Rag Dolls
hair front
page 30
Enlarge to twice
this size

Doll's Clothes
shoes
page 34
Enlarge to twice
this size

back

front

back fold

back fold

Doll's Clothes
coat
page 34
Enlarge to twice
this size

Place on fold for back

For front cut on
fold line

front fold

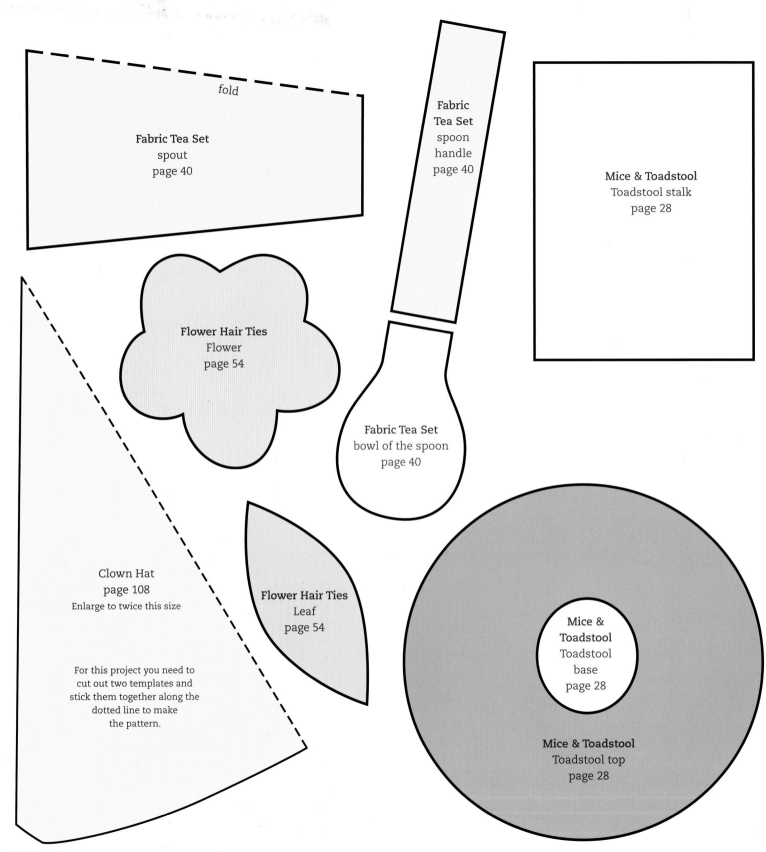

fold

Fabric Tea Set
spout
page 40

Fabric Tea Set
spoon handle
page 40

Mice & Toadstool
Toadstool stalk
page 28

Flower Hair Ties
Flower
page 54

Fabric Tea Set
bowl of the spoon
page 40

Clown Hat
page 108
Enlarge to twice this size

For this project you need to cut out two templates and stick them together along the dotted line to make the pattern.

Flower Hair Ties
Leaf
page 54

Mice & Toadstool
Toadstool base
page 28

Mice & Toadstool
Toadstool top
page 28

Suppliers

UK

Early Learning Centre
08705 352 352
www.elc.co.uk

Homecrafts Direct
0116 269 7733
www.homecrafts.co.uk

Hobbycraft
0800 027 2387
www.hobbycraft.co.uk

John Lewis
08456 049 049
www.johnlewis.co.uk

Kidzcraft
01793 327022
www.kidzcraft.co.uk

Paperchase
0161 839 1500 for mail order
www.paperchase.co.uk

Paper and String
www.paper-and-string.net

US

Art Supplies Online
800-967-7367
www.artsuppliesonline.com

Craft Site Directory
Useful online resource
www.craftsitedirectory.com

Create For Less
866-333-4463
www.createforless.com

Darice
866-432-7423
www.darice.com

Hobby Lobby
Stores nationwide
www.hobbylobby.com

Jo-ann Fabric & Crafts
888-739-4120
www.joann.com

Michaels
Stores nationwide
www.michaels.com

S&S Worldwide Craft Supplies
800-288-9941
www.ssww.com

Sunshine Crafts/Consumer
Crafts
800-729-2878
www.sunshinecrafts.com or
www.consumercrafts.com

Toys "R" Us
Stores nationwide
www.toysrus.com

Index

Acknowledgments

A very big thank you to Debbie Patterson for bringing alive the projects and always capturing the moment.

Thank you to our fabulously enthusiastic models Mohamed and Fatima Zahra Et-Taheri, Maddie Hill, Isaac and Milli Simcock-Brown, Alex and Indi Godfrey Strowbridge, and Gracie and Betty Dahl. You are all stars! And thank you to all your parents for bringing you to our shoots.

Many thanks to Pete Jorgensen for extreme patience and hard work in pulling it all together, Helen Ridge for editing, Sally Powell for organising lovely models and locations, and Cindy Richards for letting me do the book in the first place.

And thank you to Laurie, Gracie, and Betty. For everything. I couldn't have done it without you.